30 Days Praying For The Nations

Kimberly Moses

REJOICE
Essential Publishing

30 Days Praying For The Nations/ Kimberly Moses

ISBN-13: 978-1-952312-82-3

LCCN: 2021942622

Dedication

THIS BOOK WOULDN'T BE possible without the inspiration of the Holy Spirit. To all the intercessors, don't give up. Your prayers are powerful and shifts the nations. God will reward you for your faithfulness.

2 Timothy 3:16-17 says, "All scripture is given by inspiration of God, and is profitable for doctrine, for reproof, for correction, for instruction in righteousness: That the man of God may be perfect, thoroughly furnished unto all good works."

Table of Contents

Introduction

A T THE END OF 2020, the Lord began to deal with me about praying more for the Nations. Covid-19 was the cause of death for many lives world-wide. President Donald Trump refused a peaceful transfer of power, spreading conspiracy theories, dividing the church and causing hate groups to rise up. Those groups raided the US Capitol on January 6, 2021.[1] The atmosphere in the United States of America was chaotic and dark. I felt led to pray for the Nations for 30 days in my prayer group, "Intercessors That War." According to Bible Study, the number thirty means dedication to a task or a calling.[2] Jesus and I both started our ministries at 30. This number is dear to my heart because it's the age that my life forever changed.

Daily I posted an outline of prayer points that eventually became this book. The intercessors around me were dedicated to this vision of praying for the nations because they were tired of

---

1. Leatherby, Lauren, Arielle Ray, Anjali Singhvi, Christiaan Triebert, Derek Watkins, and Haley Willis. "How a Presidential Rally Turned Into a Capitol Rampage." The New York Times. January 12, 2021. Accessed May 10, 2021. https://www.nytimes.com/interactive/2021/01/12/us/capitol-mob-timeline.html.
2. "Meaning of Numbers in the BibleThe Number 30." Bible Study. Accessed May 10, 2021. https://www.biblestudy.org/bibleref/meaning-of-numbers-in-bible/30.html.

what was occurring in the land. We gathered daily at noon and cried out to God. Our prayers prepared us for what was to come as prophecy came forth and the power of God was released. We were never blind-sighted by the enemy. When we saw things happening on the news, we weren't shaken.

Proverbs 10:30 (BSB) says, "The righteous will never be shaken, but the wicked will not inhabit the land."

We truly believe that our intercession lessened the demonic blows in the Earth and canceled some of the enemy's plans. The enemy wants to destroy this land and come against the things of God. However, if the saints arise, pray, and cry out against injustice, we will see a change.

James 5:16 says, "Confess your faults one to another, and pray one for another, that ye may be healed. The effectual fervent prayer of a righteous man availeth much."

This book is designed to bring healing to the land and bring God's heart from Heaven down to earth.

2 Chronicles 7:14 says, "If my people, which are called by my name, shall humble themselves, and pray, and seek my face, and turn from their wicked ways; then will I hear from heaven, and will forgive their sin, and will heal their land."

We are required to pray and make all supplications regardless if you like or agree with an individual.

Ephesians 6:18 (NIV) says, "And pray in the Spirit on all occasions with all kinds of prayers and requests. With this in mind, be alert and always keep on praying for all the Lord's people."

1 Timothy 2:1-2 (BSB) says, "First of all, then, I urge that petitions, prayers, intercessions, and thanksgiving be offered for everyone— for kings and all those in authority—so that we may lead tranquil and quiet lives in all godliness and dignity."

This book isn't meant to demoralize any politician or leader. It is simply stating historical facts so we can learn from them and break demonic cycles. God doesn't allow any experience to go to waste. We merely examine what went wrong, pointing out the faults, and focus on what not to do. Each day focuses on a particular topic and provides points to pray for a breakthrough. Each main topic and some subtopics include scriptures and mini prayers. Use this book as a tool for your ministry, church, or meetings.

Prayer For The President, Vice-President, President-Elect, VP-Elect, Advisors, Elected officials, Senate, House of Representatives

THE PRESIDENT, VICE-PRESIDENT, PRESI-DENT-ELECT, VP-Elect, Advisors, Elected officials, Senate, House of Representatives make laws and can make things happen on many levels. Their decisions affect us locally, statewide, and federally. The passed laws can alter food safety, economy, natural environment, housing, medicine, education, entertainment, family, and so much more. I was disappointed to see the leader of the country in 2020 act in a way that wasn't fit for office. Manipulating, controlling, bullying, lying, name-calling, cursing, or violence is never okay. If you are blessed to be in a position of authority, be a good steward over it. God allowed you to be there.

Romans 13:1 (ESV) says, "Let every person be subject to the governing authorities. For there is no authority except from God, and those that exist have been instituted by God."

People are looking up to you, and you must ensure that you are impacting lives positively. Major corruption occurred during this time, which eventually got exposed, such as the severity of COVID-19, vaccines, election results, scandals, and so much more. President Trump and his team tried to downplay the Coronavirus, and a recording came out revealing it months later.[3] Many blamed him for the surge of the virus and deaths since he made wearing a mask a political statement. Masks are known to prevent breathing in contaminated air and protect the sinus from the splatter of foreign particles. Masses attended his campaign rallies without wearing masks or social distancing, which the Center for Disease Control warned against. President Trump disagreed with science and the facts, which later backfired as he and several others surrounding him contracted COVID-19.[4]

3. "Trump Tells Woodward He Deliberately Downplayed Coronavirus Threat." NPR. September 10, 2020. Accessed May 10, 2021. https://www.npr.org/2020/09/10/911368698/trump-tells-woodward-he-deliberately-downplayed-coronavirus-threat.

4. Stolberg, Sheryl Gay. "Trump and Friends Got Coronavirus Care Many Others Couldn't." The New York Times. December 10, 2020. Accessed May 10, 2021. https://www.nytimes.com/2020/12/09/us/politics/trump-coronavirus-treatments.html.

Luke 8:17 says, "For nothing is secret, that shall not be made manifest; neither any thing hid, that shall not be known and come abroad."

GODLY WISDOM

Our leaders need God's wisdom to make the best decision. They can't be sold out to money, fame, or other evil works. God's wisdom is so different from earthly wisdom. What seems like a great idea in the natural world may be contrary to God's standards. When the nation is in alignment with God, then it will be blessed.

Psalm 33:12 says, "Blessed is the nation whose God is the LORD; and the people whom he hath chosen for his own inheritance."

Dear Heavenly Father,

Please impart godly wisdom to the leaders of the country. Allow them to seek Your counsel when they make decisions. Soften their hearts to have Your plans. You said that if any man lacks wisdom, they can come to You without reproach and You will give them wisdom generously (James 1:5). Thank You for answering this prayer in Jesus' name. Amen.

HEALTH

Our leaders need to be healthier to lead effectively. It was scary to see the President of the United States and his circle contract a deadly virus. Many people worldwide and leaders of foreign countries have perished. In addition, President Joe Biden is older and many rumors are spreading that he is in the early stages of dementia. When a leader is rumored to be sick, the country is in disarray. For instance, when Kim Jong Un, the leader of North Korea, was supposedly rumored to be dead because he had surgery and wasn't seen for weeks, chaos started to emerge.[5] However, once he made an appearance to refute the claims, things became orderly again.

3 John 1:2 (ESV) says, "Beloved, I pray that all may go well with you and that you may be in good health, as it goes well with your soul."

Dear Heavenly Father,

Bless our leaders of this country to have great health and long life. If they are sick, we command healing now in the name of Jesus. Bless them to be in their right minds and not be underneath any demonic influence. Bless them to eat healthy, exercise, and take any precautions to extend their lives. Thank You for answering this prayer in Jesus' name. Amen.

SAFETY

We always need our leaders to be safe to defend against weak links in our country. Terrorist groups are always plotting their attacks. Whenever you are in a leadership position, you will be hated even though you have many supporters. People

5. "Kim Jong Un's Doctor Botched Heart Surgery as His Hands Were Shaking, Claims Report." Business Today. April 26, 2020. Accessed May 10, 2021. https://www.businesstoday.in/latest/trends/kim-jong-uns-doctor-botched-heart-surgery-as-his-hands-were-shaking-claims-report/story/402055.html.

will love and hate you at the same time. Leaders of the country need security around them, so they don't get assassinated. Since the assassination of President John F. Kennedy, security measurements have increased. Presidents don't ride around in drop top convertibles but in bulletproof cars like fully equipped Cadillacs or Lincolns.

Psalm 28:7 (ESV) says, "The Lord is my strength and my shield; in him my heart trusts, and I am helped; my heart exults, and with my song I give thanks to him.

Dear Heavenly Father,

Protect our leaders from terrorism, assassination, and death threats. Cover their transportation and the foods that they eat. Bless them to have the best medical care to do their jobs effectively. Bless the people around them to have discernment to scan the environment for danger. Thank You for answering this prayer in Jesus' name. Amen.

HUMILITY

Our leaders need to be humble as it was the Lord that allowed them to be in this position. Those that are prideful will eventually stumble. King Nebuchadnezzar was very prideful and ate grass in the field for seven years. It wasn't until he acknowledged God and praised Him that his mind was restored (Daniel 4:25-35). President Donald Trump was very boastful, especially during his speeches. It was sad to see him fall. He has financial troubles, claims of tax frauds, and some of his businesses and estates are on the verge of bankruptcy.[6]

Proverbs 16:18 says, "Pride goeth before destruction, and an haughty spirit before a fall."

Dear Heavenly Father,

Bless our leaders to stay humble because You will give grace unto them. However, if they are prideful, You will oppose them. Bless the leaders to be teachable and to remember the small beginnings. Allow them to relate and fight for those who are overlooked in society. Thank You for answering this prayer in Jesus' name. Amen.

INTEGRITY

Our leaders need to walk in integrity to rid themselves of any corruption. When a politician is corrupt, they will sway for money and won't stand up and fight for the people that elected them in that office. Also, they will lack character and engage in conduct that is against God and their oath of office. We don't need another scandal among politicians. It's shameful and embarrassing for our nation.

Proverbs 10:9 (ESV) says, "Whoever walks in integrity walks securely, but he who makes his ways crooked will be found out."

Dear Heavenly Father,

___

6. "Debt Cloud Hangs over Trump Post-presidency | TheHill." Accessed May 10, 2021. https://thehill.com/policy/finance/534588-debt-cloud-hangs-over-trump-post-presidency.

Bless the leaders of this nation to walk on the straight and narrow path. If they aren't saved, bless them with an opportunity for them to give their lives to Jesus Christ. Soften their hard hearts and draw them close to You. Bless them always to do the right thing when no one is looking. Thank You for answering this prayer in Jesus' name. Amen.

GUIDANCE

Some of our politicians are surrounded by bad counsel. They don't need to be 'yes' men who only speak what the politician wants to hear. These council members need to speak the truth so the leader can make sound decisions that are beneficial for all they govern. Our political leaders need counsel from those who are godly yet skilled in their field of expertise.

Psalm 32:8 (ESV) says, "I will instruct you and teach you in the way you should go; I will counsel you with my eye upon you."

Dear Heavenly Father,

Allow our political leaders to have an ear to hear Your voice in the counsel around them. Order their steps and send Your servants in their paths to make an impact in their lives. Bless our leaders to seek Your face and acknowledge You in every way so You can direct their paths.

UNITER NOT A DIVIDER

In North America, our government is divided into several branches and divisions. However, whoever is elected should unite the nation's people for the common good, especially during tragic times. A real leader knows how to lead and become a solutionist. We have witnessed enough name-calling and finger-pointing in the COVID-19 pandemic. Now it's time to come together and heal.

Psalm 133:1 (ESV) says, "Behold, how good and pleasant it is when brothers dwell in unity!"

Dear Heavenly Father,

You are love and command us to love our neighbors as we love ourselves. Bless those in leadership to love those who don't look like them, from different backgrounds, economic class, or political parties. Bless the leader not to stir up hate or racism. Bless the leaders to condemn violence and stand up for righteousness. Thank You for answering this prayer in Jesus' name. Amen.

SALVATION/DELIVERANCE

God has His people in government so they can do His will in the political system. There are so many demonic laws and decrees being passed. God needs His servants crying aloud. Our political leaders need to be saved and delivered by the power of the Lord Jesus Christ. We have witnessed the crime rates and immorality increase in this nation as some wicked politicians fought to remove God out of the equation. As a result, perversion is forced upon this generation and school shootings have been a common thing.

Romans 10:9 (ESV) says, "Because, if you confess with your mouth that Jesus is Lord and believe in your heart that God raised him from the dead, you will be saved."

Dear Heavenly Father,

You know how to bring us out of darkness and transform us into the marvelous light of Your dear Son Jesus Christ. You don't desire for anyone to perish. Bless our politicians to be saved and delivered. Allow them to confess their sins and repent of any wickedness. I pray that they won't be an enemy to the cross but a friend. I pray they are open to receiving Jesus in their hearts. God send Your power and Word to breakthrough and transform the hardest hearts for Your glory. Thank You for answering this prayer in Jesus' name. Amen.

DO WHAT'S BEST FOR PEOPLE

Sometimes a politician may start off right but later become corrupt by the system. They allow money to be their motivating factor and will be easily brought by greedy corporations. As a result, they pass laws or vote in favor of the corporation instead of the people or the environment. For instance, imagine a chemical plant located in a poor area. The waste is causing those in the community to get cancer. There are numerous lawsuits and medical documentation, but the politicians don't use their power or influence to pass restrictions against the chemical plant because they are being compensated or receiving gifts from the plant. Our leaders must not support unjust laws or turn a blind eye to it. It's not God's will for the poor to become poorer and the rich to become richer due to unfair taxes imposed on the less fortunate while the rich receive tax breaks.

Hebrews 13:16 says, "Do not neglect to do good and to share what you have, for such sacrifices are pleasing to God."

Dear Heavenly Father,

Bless our politicians to have a heart for the people. Protect their heart against greed, lust, fame, and every evil work. Allow them to fight for those who have no voice or influence. Bless them to be an advocate for the poor. Deliver them from fear of man because it brings a snare. Thank You for answering this prayer in Jesus' name. Amen.

MENTALLY STABLE

Our leaders of the country need to have mental stability. Donald Trump's last weeks in office were gut-wrenching because he went on a firing spree. Everyone that disagreed with him concerning the election results he terminated them regardless of their experience or how long they were on that job. He was in denial and posted on Twitter that he won the election by a lot even after Joe Biden was declared the winner of the election. People started to question if Donald Trump was fit for office and wanted to invoke the 25th amendment.[7]

2 Corinthians 10:5 says, "Casting down imaginations, and every high thing that exalteth itself against the knowledge of God, and bringing into captivity every thought to the obedience of Christ;"

7. Drescher, Jack. "On the 25th Amendment and Donald Trump: Don't Weaponize Psychiatry." Psychiatric News 56, no. 3 (2021). doi:10.1176/appi.pn.2021.3.37.

Dear Heavenly Father,

Allow our leaders to be in their right minds so they can govern effectively. Bless them to renew their minds so they won't be conformed to the ways of the world. I decree that the same mind that is in Jesus Christ will be upon our politicians. Thank You for answering this prayer in Jesus' name. Amen.

KINGDOM CITIZENS

Many people feel like they have to be behind the pulpit to do ministry. However, God can call His people into government and that system is a part of their ministry. There are plenty of people in politics that are not saved and need a Savior, Jesus Christ. Kingdom citizens can't be bought or sold out for any money, gift, or incentive. They won't lose their souls for pleasure. They will remain on God's side regardless of what political party they represent.

John 18:36 (ESV) says, "Jesus answered, "My kingdom is not of this world. If my kingdom were of this world, my servants would have been fighting, that I might not be delivered over to the Jews. But my kingdom is not from the world."

Dear Heavenly Father,

Send Your services into the political system to make a great impact for Your glory. Lord, promotion doesn't come from man but from You. You demote one and raise up another. Send Kingdom citizens to replace agents of Satan so Your agenda can be done in our government. Thank You for answering this prayer in Jesus' name. Amen.

GOVERN WELL

Not everyone has the gift of leadership. We can review the track record of various events in history and see countless mistakes made jeopardizing the lives of those they led. God can ensure that we are prosperous and make the best decisions that will cause our nation to succeed. God gave Joseph strategies for the famine so Egypt and surrounding nations wouldn't perish (Genesis 41). However, if the leader is selfish and for themselves, others will suffer. Leadership must seek God to govern well.

James 3:16 (ESV) says, "For where jealousy and selfish ambition exist, there will be disorder and every vile practice."

Dear Heavenly Father,

Bless our leaders to seek Your face so they will govern well. I bind up selfishness and every evil work in Jesus' name. Allow our leaders to consider the needs of others when voting and passing laws. Bless our leaders to have mentors and to learn from history's mistakes so they don't repeat them. Thank you for answering this prayer in Jesus' name. Amen.

UPHOLD THE LAW

Our leaders aren't above the law, but they have been elected to uphold it. They must respect and honor the constitution.

Bending the rules to get ahead should never happen. Since these leaders are in position, a higher standard must be raised. God judges His leaders with a stricter standard. No one gets away with anything. Eventually, their sins catch up to them, exposure occurs, and they stumble.

James 3:1 (NKJV) says, "My brethren, let not many of you become teachers, knowing that we shall receive a stricter judgment."

Dear Heavenly Father,

You are a God of order and not the author of confusion. You are fair and just. Bless our leaders not to compromise but to uphold the law. If there are any demonic laws, overturn them and allow laws to be passed that align with your will. Thank You for answering this prayer in Jesus' name. Amen.

NO COMPETITION

Even though our government is divided, they still must learn how to put their differences aside to pass policy. In 2020, the government was so divided that people couldn't get help. People's unemployment benefits were on the verge of running out. Many were hungry, evicted, and didn't know how to survive. It took congress many months to pass a second stimulus check. There was an agenda attached to certain bills preventing the other party from agreeing with it. As a result, many people suffered.

Mark 3:25 says, "And if a house be divided against itself, that house cannot stand."

Dear Heavenly Father,

Allow our leaders of this nation to work together so people can get the help that they need. Bless the environment to be peaceful and full of Your love. Bless these politicians to put their agenda down and pick up yours. I bind up the spirit of division and hatred in Jesus' name. Amen.

FEAR OF THE LORD IN THEIR HEARTS

The leaders of the nations need to be friends of God. God needs His people in the governmental system, so they don't sin against Him. Politics can get ugly at times, but there is no need to curse, cheat, lie, manipulate, or control others. When the leaders get the fear of the Lord in their hearts, God's will can come down to earth.

Job 28:28 (ESV) says, "And he said to man,'Behold, the fear of the Lord, that is wisdom, and to turn away from evil is understanding.'"

Dear Heavenly Father,

Allow our political leaders to be in awe of You, so Your fear can be in their hearts. You bless us with wisdom when we ask for it, so allow our politicians to cry out for godly wisdom and understanding. Bless our politicians to shun evil and seek righteousness. Thank You for answering this prayer in Jesus' name. Amen.

DAY 2

Pray for the Justice System, Judges, and Attorneys

THE JUDICIAL SYSTEM NEEDS our prayers because it's role is to decide the meaning of laws and their application. The judicial branch interprets the constitution and can limit the power of the other branches of government: Legislative and executive. If anyone gets out of line, the judicial branch can set order. There has been demonic infiltration where Judges allow Satanic prayer and rule unjustly.[8] Some attorneys are money hungry, liars, and manipulators. Our prayers can bombard the courtroom and cause change. We can see the hand of the Lord move and justice prevail on our behalf.

RIGHTEOUS JUDGES

---

8. Norton, Jasmine Anderson / Allie. "Satanic Prayer at Council Meeting Disrupted by Crowd." WEAR. July 21, 2016. Accessed July 06, 2021. https://weartv.com/news/local/satanic-prayer-at-council-meeting-disrupted-by-crowd.

Men will make mistakes and can learn from the best Judge, God. When the wrong person is in position, they will fight for things that are contrary to God's Word. These judges will impose unjust laws because their conscience is seared. Our judges need a sound mind and a good conscience to deliver decisions based on biblical and moral values.

Psalm 89:14 says, "Righteousness and justice are the foundation of your throne; steadfast love and faithfulness go before you."

Dear Heavenly Father,

Bless the judges in our nation to be just and rule righteously. Allow them to seek You after they have heard cases so they can give the right sentences. Bless them to have a relationship with You and grow in the knowledge of Jesus Christ. Bless the laws to be just. Amen.

WORKERS OF RIGHTEOUSNESS

The workers of the judicial branch need to legislate the heart and mind of God upon the earth. Workers of righteousness are led by God's Spirit and uphold the Word of God as a standard. They aren't corrupt and they shun evil. They also have integrity.

1 Peter 1:17 says, "...Father who judges impartially according to each one's deeds..."

Dear Heavenly Father,

Save and deliver the people in the judicial branch. Allow them to be a light in a dark place. Bless them to be a witness for You and love those who they cross paths with. Bless them never to be ashamed to talk about You or Your Son Jesus. Allow them to fight against corruption and take a stand for righteousness' sake in Jesus' name. Amen.

NO PREJUDICE

America has a racist past. During the 1955 murder trial of Emmett Till, a young black boy brutally murder for whistling at a white woman, his family had to stand before an all white jury and judge. These jurors and the judge were full of hate and allowed two murderers to get away. The white woman who lied on Emmett Till later came forth and admitted that she lied.[9] Imagine if there weren't any prejudice during that time, justice would have been served.

Deuteronomy 10:17 (NKJV), "God...who shows no partiality nor takes a bribe."

Dear Heavenly Father,

Bless the jurors, judges, and those in the judicial system not to be prejudiced. We bind up the spirit of hatred and strife. Loose Your love in the courtroom and penetrate every hard heart. Allow justice to prevail so the families and loved ones

9. "Emmett Till." n.d. Biography. Accessed May 10, 2021. https://www.biography.com/crime-figure/emmett-till#:~:text=Murder%20Trial.

of the victims can have their day of victory in the court. Thank You for answering this prayer in Jesus' name. Amen.

NO SOCIAL INEQUALITY

There have been hundreds of cases where people were arrested and charged with crimes that they didn't commit. Some of these charges were racially motivated. Years later, DNA exonerated some and the prisoner was compensated financially. However, in some cases, they weren't rewarded as much as they deserved for their pain and suffering. Race, social status, or religious background should not be used against the person who is facing a trial. Trials must be fair.

Leviticus 19:15 (ESV) says, "You shall do no injustice in court. You shall not be partial to the poor or defer to the great, but in righteousness shall you judge your neighbor."

Dear Heavenly Father,

Bless those who work in the judicial system not to be biased or discriminate against those who don't look like them or come from a different background. Let those who serve in this branch of government be truthful and honor the vow they made before you in the court of law. Let them not fight against truth or righteousness even if it means that they will lose their case. Thank you for answering this prayer in Jesus' name. Amen.

NO ATTACKS ON OUR RELIGIOUS FREEDOM

The First Amendment in the US Constitution gives us the right to religious freedom. However, many cases have been tried in court around this issue. The judge must determine the impact of an individual's rights and apply the First Amendment on the defendant's behalf. Christians are often brought to court because of their beliefs. The Judge must not be biased but allow believers in Jesus Christ to serve God without persecution from lawmakers and enemies of the cross.

Galatians 5:1 (ESV) says, "For freedom Christ has set us free; stand firm therefore, and do not submit again to a yoke of slavery."

Dear Heavenly Father,

Bless the lawmakers not to attack others based on their religious beliefs. Allow those in the judicial system to uphold the First Amendment and Your Word. Bless the jurors and judges to judge righteously. Soft the hearts of the persecutors and the plaintiffs in Jesus' name. Amen.

SHUN EVIL AND EXPOSE IT

Often we see a radical new leader come on the scene who exposes corruptness in the system while promising change. God will open doors for His servants to go through the process of being vetted and selected to fill certain seats. The judicial system workers need boldness to do the right thing and not become part of the problem of a corrupt system but be a solutionist.

1 Peter 3:11 (NKJV) says, "Let him turn away from evil and do good; Let him seek peace and pursue it."

Dear Heavenly Father,

Bless those in the judicial system to be bold and if needed to go against the grain even when it's not popular. Bless them not to worry about their career ending due to threats. Bless and protect them for standing in truth and departing from evil. Give them strength and peace as they expose darkness in Jesus' name. Amen.

ADVOCATE TO THOSE WITH NO VOICE

Some people in the judicial system are advocates for those who have no voice. They will take cases pro-bono or become public defenders. It's not all about the money for these people, but they are passionate about what they are doing. They find fulfillment in helping others because it's their life's call. Advocates are voices for the poor, needy, widow, or overlooked.

1 John 2:1 (ESV) says, "My little children, I am writing these things to you so that you may not sin. But if anyone does sin, we have an advocate with the Father, Jesus Christ the righteous."

Dear Heavenly Father,

Bless those in the judicial system to be an advocate to those who aren't being heard and taken advantage of by corruption. Order their steps and bless them with the tools and support they need to take down Satan or evil agents in Jesus Christ's name. Amen.

PROTECTION

Sometimes when someone takes on cases, they will receive threats and intimidation from others. Often their family is in danger. A lawyer was gunned down at his home by someone pretending to be a delivery man. Days later, a federal judge's son was murdered as he opened the door when someone rang the bell.[10] These were heinous crimes and shouldn't be a reality to those who serve our government. They need God's protection as they are doing their assignment.

Psalm 91:11 says, "For he shall give his angels charge over thee, to keep thee in all thy ways."

Dear Heavenly Father,

Protect those in the judicial system and their families. Bless them to always be at the right place at the right time. We bind up death threats and terrorism in the name of Jesus. Give your angels charge over them and bless them to dwell underneath the shadow of your wings in Jesus' name. Amen.

GODLY WISDOM

---

10. "Federal Judge Whose Son Was Killed in Ambush: 'My Son's Death Cannot Be in Vain.'" n.d. Www.cbsnews.com. Accessed May 10, 2021. https://www.cbsnews.com/news/esther-salas-son-murder-roy-den-hollander-48-hours/.

God's wisdom is different from worldly wisdom. His wisdom is pure, peaceable, no hypocrisy, and merciful. When we have godly wisdom, there won't be any demonic backlash involved because God has already given us foresight. When a judge can't rule properly, their decision can be challenged up to the Supreme Court, which is deemed the highest court in the land.

James 3:17 (BLB) says, "But the wisdom from above is indeed first pure, then peaceable, gentle, reasonable, full of mercy and of good fruits, impartial, sincere."

Dear Heavenly Father,

Bless those in the judicial system not to make mistakes of law. Bless them with Your wisdom so things won't grow increasingly worse or cause more harm than good. Bless these leaders to have common sense and thoroughly do their research before ruling. Allow everyone involved to do their part and seek You for counsel. Thank You for answering this prayer in Jesus' name. Amen.

KINGDOM CITIZENS TO FILL THESE POSITIONS

God promotes others while demoting others. He can shake wickedness out of the earth and the government. Some Judges that are in position are for God's people and opposed abomination. God's people aren't ashamed of the faith even when people come against them. Kingdom citizens have a reverence for God.

Hebrews 12:28 (ESV) says, "Therefore let us be grateful for receiving a kingdom that cannot be shaken, and thus let us offer to God acceptable worship, with reverence and awe,"

Dear Heavenly Father,

Your Kingdom will never be shaken. Bless the workers of the judicial system to serve You with reverence and awe. Send the replacements as you did with David replacing Saul. Give your servants courage and strength to do Your will in Jesus' name. Amen.

Military: Army, Navy, Air Force, Marines and Coast Guard.

O UR MILITARY NEEDS PRAYER. There are wars and crises worldwide. Our military is a force that keeps things in order and peaceful. They must have the best technology to advance over the enemy. In the COVID-19 pandemic, we saw much civil unrest, protest, and domestic terrorism. The military was called to keep order in the streets. God has bestowed double honor upon them because of their service. One of the ways we honor our military is Veterans and Memorial Day.

STRONG

2 Timothy 2:3 (NKJV) says, "You therefore must endure hardship as a good soldier of Jesus Christ."

Our soldiers must be strong even when it means suffering. Not all soldiers are bad people. Some are believers in Jesus, and have family. They must show great courage when facing their enemies.

Dear Heavenly Father,

Bless our military to be strong and stand together during the battle. Give them comfort and let them know that You are with them. Allow them to set their faces like a flint and not show any signs of weakness. Thank You for answering this prayer in Jesus Christ's name. Amen.

HEALTHY

3 John 2 says, "Beloved, I wish above all things that thou mayest prosper and be in health, even as thy soul prospereth."

Our soldiers need to be healthy so they can serve and protect our country. Sometimes they might be in harsh environments such as deserts, swamps, or rocky terrain. Their immune system must be built up to handle adverse weather and travel. If they are sickly, then their bodies won't be able to adjust to changes in climate.

Dear Heavenly Father,

Bless our military to be healthy. Protect them from being guinea pigs or being experimented on with new drugs or vaccines. Bless their immune system to be strong to fight off any infections and diseases. Allow them to eat healthy, sleep well, and maintain their strenuous exercise requirements. Thank you for answering this prayer in Jesus Christ's name. Amen.

MORAL UPRIGHTNESS

Our military needs to do the right thing when no one is looking. When they travel to other countries, the laws may be different, which opens them up to sin such as sex, alcohol, false religion, etc. They must say no to evil even when everyone else around them is partaking in it. For instance, some countries have brothels and prostitution is common. Our soldiers need to have self-control to not give in to their flesh.

Proverbs 14:2 (NASB) says, "He who walks in his uprightness fears the Lord, But he who is devious in his ways despises Him."

Dear Heavenly Father,

Bless our military to have the fear of the Lord in their hearts. Bless them to have godly character and follow You with everything within them. Bless them to have a relationship with You and not be ashamed to be a light in dark places. Thank You for answering this prayer in Jesus' name. Amen.

FINISH THEIR TASK

Our military needs knowledge and skill to operate machinery, technology, aircraft, and weaponry. They must not quit when things get hard. They must show mental strength regardless of the challenges they face. They have to realize that many people around the world are depending on them to protect and serve. They must excel at their jobs because so much is at stake.

Galatians 6:9 (NIV) says, "Let us not become weary in doing good, for at the proper time we will reap a harvest if we do not give up."

Dear Heavenly Father,

Bless our military not to be weary in well-doing but continue on their assignments. Bless them to persevere and endure the task before them. Bless them to walk in the spirit of excellence. Allow them to be imitators of Jesus as He with joy endured the cross. Strengthen our soldiers, Lord. Thank You for answering this prayer in Jesus' name. Amen.

BRAVE

Many soldiers have died on the battlefield and some while on duty outside of war. They must realize that they are one of the first lines of defense against any enemies of the country. Even when they are scared, they must look to heaven and know that God has not given them the spirit of fear.

2 Timothy 1:7 says, "For God has not given us a spirit of fear, but of power and of love and of a sound mind."

Dear Heavenly Father,

You commanded us many times in Your Word to be bold and courageous. You are more powerful than the enemy. When we are weak, You are strong. Bless our soldiers to defeat every Goliath that stands before them. Bless every mountain in the paths to be removed. Thank You for answering this prayer in Jesus' name. Amen.

PROTECTION

There have been many wars since biblical times resulting in much bloodshed. People have always sought the Lord for His protection and it shouldn't be any different than today. God will cancel the hidden attacks that we can't see. He will warn us of the enemy's plans so we can be one step ahead. Our soldiers need divine insight and discernment.

2 Corinthians 1:10 (ESV) says, "He delivered us from such a deadly peril, and he will deliver us. On him we have set our hope that he will deliver us again."

Dear Heavenly Father,

Protect our soldiers on the battlefield. Please provide deliverance if they are being held captive by the enemy. Never allow them to be a casualty of war. Keep them safe from terrorism. Place a supernatural hedge of protection around them. Bless them with discernment. Thank You for answering this prayer in Jesus' name. Amen.

MENTAL STABILITY

Some soldiers have PTSD or post-traumatic stress disorder due to everything they have experienced. Some suffer from nightmares and withdraw from loved ones and family. Little things can be triggers and can lead to alcoholism, violence, and depression. God can renew their minds and help them overcome mental disorders. Our soldiers must make the right decision for our country and mental instability will hinder this. Mental issues will have soldiers breaking laws.

2 Corinthians 10:5 says, "Casting down imaginations, and every high thing that exalteth itself against the knowledge of God, and bringing into captivity every thought to the obedience of Christ;"

Dear Heavenly Father,

Bless our military to have mental stability. Deliver them from nightmares, depression, alcoholism, emotional triggers, any forms of abuse, violence, anger, and withdrawal symptoms. Bless them to get counseling and seek You Lord for hope and peace. Bless their families with patience and support as they heal and move forward in challenging times. Thank You for answering this prayer in Jesus' name. Amen.

FAMILY LIFE

Our soldiers need to learn how to adapt to home life when they come back from tour. Also, their families need to adapt to their traveling. Divorce rates may be higher since the soldier may be away for a long time while on duty. Their spouses must be faithful while they are away. Our soldiers need prayer for their families. They need to return home to a stable environment. Also, we need to pray that God comforts the families who have lost a loved one serving in the military.

Psalm 133:1 (NKJV) says, "How good and pleasant it is when God's people live together in unity!"

Dear Heavenly Father,

Bless our soldiers to come back to a peaceful and stable environment. Allow their families and loved ones to be welcoming. We bind up any demonic attacks in their homes and marriages. Allow the families of the soldier to be kind, loving, and adaptive to change. Unify the family and strengthen their unit. Comfort those who are hurting and grieving. Thanks for answering this prayer in Jesus Christ's name. Amen.

HOPE IN JESUS

Our soldiers need to place their hope in Jesus for sanity, peace, and protection. Their assignments may be challenging, but with Jesus, they can get through them. When they feel lonely and miss their families, they can find comfort in the Lord. When they are afraid, they can trust in God that everything will be okay one day.

Isaiah 40:31 (NIV) says, "but those who hope in the LORD will renew their strength. They will soar on wings like eagles; they will run and not grow weary, they will walk and not faint."

Dear Heavenly Father,

Bless our soldiers to have hope in You. Don't allow them to lose hope because hope deferred makes the heart sick. Bless them to keep going when they want to give up. Allow them to keep fighting the good fight of faith. Bless them to depend on You and realize that Jesus is their rock. Thank You for answering this prayer in Jesus' name. Amen.

PEACE

Our soldiers need the peace of God because their jobs can be stressful at times. God will keep our soldiers in perfect peace so they won't panic or fall apart. God will surround our soldiers in peace in their coming and going. It is not the will of God for our soldiers to be on medication for anxiety and depression.

Philippians 4:6-7 says, "Do not be anxious about anything, but in every situation, by prayer and petition, with thanksgiving, present your requests to God. And the peace of God, which transcends all understanding, will guard your hearts and your minds in Christ Jesus."

Dear Heavenly Father,

Bless our soldiers to focus on You and keep their minds stayed on Jesus so they can have perfect peace. Bless them not to be anxious about anything because there is nothing too hard for You. Bless these soldiers to know that they can trust You and that You can do the impossible. Thank You for answering this prayer in Jesus' name. Amen.

FINANCIAL WISDOM

Our military needs financial wisdom on every level. They need the tools and resources to win every battle and have the best equipment and technology. Debts can be a hindrance and stressful. The military needs to be wise with their money. I have witnessed some soldiers carelessly spend their paychecks in the clubs and are hungry until their next paycheck.

Dear Heavenly Father,

Bless our soldiers to be good financial stewards and not to spend their finances recklessly. Allow them to be faithful in their tithes and offerings. Bless them to sow into Your Kingdom and not spend funds on things that promote evil. Thank You for answering this prayer in Jesus' name. Amen.

Police Force

I N THE COVID-19 PANDEMIC, a lot of police brutality became exposed. The people had enough of the abuse of power that had been around for decades. There have been horror stories of policemen lynching black people or turning a blind eye so angry whites could commit acts of violence. God has allowed some issues to come to the forefront to be addressed and we could heal then move forward. There isn't a lot of trust between some members of the community and the police due to corruptness and years of injustice. God can rebuild this relationship and bring healing and reconciliation. There is now talk and laws being passed of police reformation. We must pray for the police force during these times of transition.

NO RACIAL PROFILING

Police have been profiling drivers for many years. If certain groups drove a nice car, they would be pulled over and their vehicles searched for drugs. Sometimes, these incidents ended up in murder, such as the case of George Floyd. He begged the officers to let up because he couldn't breathe while an officer kneeled on his neck.[11] As a result, he died and many uproars erupted worldwide.

John 7:24 (ESV) says, "Do not judge by appearances, but judge with right judgement."

Dear Heavenly Father,

Bless our officers to do the right thing. If they are racist, send conviction into their hearts so they can repent and get in right standing with you. Allow the police force to protect and serve not to murder by abusing their authority. Bless the officers to be delivered of fear of certain ethnicities to eliminate racial profiling. Thank You for answering this prayer in Jesus Christ's name. Amen.

NO BRUTALITY

Some police officers have been using excessive force and breaking the laws. For instance, some will intentionally rough someone up as they arrest them, tase them, and even shoot them. It doesn't always take violent tactics to make an arrest because some people will automatically comply. When excessive force is used as a method of agitation, the crooked police will band together and lie that the person was resisting arrest. These corrupt officers will take the power of the badge into their own hands and take advantage of the system. Funds are needed to provide training and develop better protocols.

---

11. Hill, Evan. 2020. "How George Floyd Was Killed in Police Custody." The New York Times, May 31, 2020, sec. U.S. https://www.nytimes.com/2020/05/31/us/george-floyd-investigation.html.

Matthew 7:1-2 (ESV) says, "Judge not, that you be not judged. For with the judgment you pronounce you will be judged, and with the measure you use it will be measured to you."

Dear Heavenly Father,

Bless the police force to not use excessive force unnecessarily. Deliver our officers from violence, anger, pride, and pain. Bless them to treat others as they want to be treated. Give them wisdom to make an arrest effectively without someone dying or becoming severely injured. Allow them to get the training that is required to up root any crookedness in the system. Thank You for answering this prayer in Jesus' name. Amen.

UPRIGHT

Not all police officers are bad. God has some of His children on the force. They pray daily and trust God for protection. They even make tough decisions to expose crime within the police system and go against corruptness even if they are threatened in various ways. Our police force needs to be upright so they won't bend under pressure and do the right thing every time. These officers are connected to the Holy Spirit to feel conviction because they have a godly conscience. God can purge the police force from evil workers.

Isaiah 26:7 (NASB) says, "The way of the righteous is smooth; O Upright One, make the path of the righteous level."

Dear Heavenly Father,

Bless our officers not to be corrupt and enable them to fight against it. Allow them to fight against crime and never cheat the system. Give them the courage to expose threats before it becomes a severe danger. Bless them to hear Your voice and trust You to order their steps. Thank You for answering this prayer in Jesus' name. Amen.

PROTECTION

Our police need our protection. Hatred of police has led to harm and fatalities. So many officers have died while on duty. Daily police put their lives on the line to serve and protect. They are the first line of defense and our first responders in an emergency. In Florence, South Carolina, two officers were dispatched with a warrant to search the home of a suspected child abuser and were ultimately killed during a shootout.[12] Our police force needs discernment to avoid harm.

Psalm 3:3 says, "But You, O LORD, are a shield about me. My glory and the One who lifts my head."

Dear Heavenly Father,

---

12. Reports, Staff and wire. n.d. "Death Penalty Sought in Florence Case Where 7 SC Officers Were Shot, 2 Fatally." Post and Courier. Accessed May 10, 2021. https://www.postandcourier.com/news/death-penalty-sought-in-florence-case-where-7-sc-officers-were-shot-2-fatally/article_787386e0-acb4-11ea-8b77-93b85b6e72cf.html#:~:text=Florence%20Police%20Sgt..

Place a hedge of protection around our officers as they serve and protect. Bless them to be safe from stray bullets, bombs, car accidents, and tragedies. Warn them when things will go wrong and danger is looming. Bless them with discernment so they can avoid being injured and killed while on duty. Bless their workplace and families to be protected from angry rioters and domestic terrorists. Thank You for answering this prayer in Jesus' name.

BRAVE

The police force must be brave, especially during assaults. On January 6, 2021, the Capitol was raided by white supremacist groups and Donald Trump supporters. These groups were mad over the election results. Some officers did their best to resist the angry mob and some died while protecting the people they swore to serve.[13] They did their jobs well despite the criticism. The Capitol raid was a scary experience for many officers because they never experienced an angry mob of that magnitude.

Deuteronomy 31:6 (NIV) says, "Be strong and courageous. Do not be afraid or terrified because of them, for the LORD your God goes with you; he will never leave you nor forsake you."

Dear Heavenly Father,

---

13. Leatherby, Lauren, Arielle Ray, Anjali Singhvi, Christiaan Triebert, Derek Watkins, and Haley Willis. 2021. "How a Presidential Rally Turned into a Capitol Rampage." The New York Times, January 12, 2021, sec. U.S. https://www.nytimes.com/interactive/2021/01/12/us/capitol-mob-timeline.html.

Bless our officers to be brave and to set their faces like a flint. Allow them to stand strong as they face their enemies. Bless the officers to stand together and be their brother's keeper. We bind up fear and intimidation off of them. Anoint them to be more than a conqueror through Jesus Christ. Amen.

WISDOM AND INTELLIGENCE

Our officers need wisdom so they can make the best choices. They also need intelligence so they can do their job in excellence. They need great problem solving skills, especially during a crisis or in an emergency. Our officers must be quick on their feet because many people depend on them to protect them. They need to hear the still small voice of the Holy Spirit in everything that they do.

James 3:13 (NIV) says, "Who is wise and understanding among you? Let them show it by their good life, by deeds done in the humility that comes from wisdom."

Dear Heavenly Father,

Bless our officers with wisdom and intelligence so they can do their job in excellence. If they lack wisdom, bless them to cry out to You for it because You will give them generous amounts of it without reproach. Bless them to hear Your voice God and draw near to You for insight. Thank You for answering this prayer in Jesus' name. Amen.

PEACE AND ENCOURAGEMENT

Our officers need God's peace so they won't be anxious or agitated by the stress that they encounter each day. God's peace will guard their hearts and minds, especially when they witness tragic events. The officers don't need to take their work home with them because it can affect their families negatively. God's peace will help the officers not give in to the temptation of drugs or alcohol. Every once in a while, the police force needs to be encouraged and reminded how vital they are to the community.

2 Corinthians 13:11 says, "Finally, brothers and sisters, rejoice! Strive for full restoration, encourage one another, be of one mind, live in peace. And the God of love and peace will be with you."

Dear Heavenly Father,

Bless our officers to be encouraged and have great peace. Bless them with peace that surpasses all understanding. When they can't see a positive outcome of the challenges they face, encourage them. Bless them to know that You are with them and will never forsake them. Thank You for answering this prayer in Jesus' name. Amen.

SALVATION AND DELIVERANCE

God has some of His children on the police force. They are called to be a light in dark places. God placed a desire in their hearts to do that line of work. God has appointed them to protect and serve others. These officers can be a witness for the

Lord Jesus and bring salvation, deliverance and healing to their fellow co-workers. There needs to be believers in Jesus Christ in all arenas.

Romans 10:9 (ESV) says, "Because, if you confess with your mouth that Jesus is Lord and believe in your heart that God raised him from the dead, you will be saved."

Dear Heavenly Father,

Bless our officers to be saved and delivered. If they don't know You as Lord and Savior, place opportunities in their paths to do so. Bless those who are saved to be a light in dark places and walk worthy of You Lord. Allow your servants to be faithful and zealous for You. Thank You for answering this prayer in Jesus' name. Amen.

PRAYER FOR FAMILIES

1 Timothy 2:1 (ESV) says, "First of all, then, I urge that supplications, prayers, intercessions, and thanksgivings be made for all people."

The families of police members need prayers too. They often have to sacrifice by giving up time they could spend with their police members by allowing them to do their jobs when duty calls. They need peace and comfort, so they don't have to stress and worry if their loved one is okay. In times of tragedy, God will comfort those who are grieving and hurting over the loss of their deceased colleague.

Dear Heavenly Father,

We lift up the family of the police force. Bless them with peace so they won't have to worry if their loved one is okay. Bless them not to resent their loved ones for working often. We bind up divorce, strife, and substance abuse in the homes. We pray that the children will be respectful and listen to both parents. We pray that the officers' home will be a safe haven after a long hard day of work. Thank You for answering this prayer in Jesus' name. Amen.

Peace

OUR NATION NEEDS PEACE because without it, there will be a spirit of lawlessness running around as never before. In the COVID-19 pandemic, a lot of wounds were uncovered and topics began to get addressed. We saw a surge of the Black Lives Matter movement and racist injustices began to get highlighted. These issues caused riots globally. Some riots ended deadly and others had a great outcome. Jesus is the Prince of Peace (Isaiah 9:6) and we are called to be peacemakers (Matthew 5:9) despite what others are doing in the world.

UNITY

God desires unity among his people. The saddest thing in the pandemic was the division in the church. Some people were torn over the election and they cut people off. One of my mentees got offended at me because I told her what the Lord put on my heart. I said, "People have gotten so distracted, fighting over the elections while the enemy's agenda is being manifested. There is a lying spirit among the prophets due to their idolatry." Everyone has a right to their opinion and it's disheartening how easily some cut off relationships due to offense. We need to work together and move forward after tragedies. We need to support one another.

1 Corinthians 1:10 (ESV) says, "I appeal to you, brothers, by the name of our Lord Jesus Christ, that all of you agree, and that there be no divisions among you, but that you be united in the same mind and the same judgment."

Dear Heavenly Father,

Bless your body not to be divided. Allow us to be unified and stand together in the faith. We have an enemy in the spirit that is doing his best to kill, steal, and destroy (John 10:10) Kingdom relationships. We need You Lord as never before to turn the hard hearts and allow them to receive Your peace. Thank you for answering this prayer in Jesus' name.

NO RACISM

1 John 4:8 (ESV) says, "Anyone who does not love does not know God, because God is love."

God has a way of using the weak things of the world to confound the mighty (1 Corinthians 1:27). For centuries, African Americans were looked down upon and not even considered human. Now, we see justice and new doors open for this ethnic group as history is being made right before our eyes. As the first Black female elected as the Vice President of the United States of America, many became upset. I shared a portrait of her and congratulated her on her victory on social media. The response was appalling from some. I also remember years ago when Barack Obama became the first Black President of the United States of America, some of my co-workers began to manifest. They wrote the N word on the bathroom wall in our work department and the work environment was very tense. Whether you agree or not, we still have to pray for those in office as our Christian duty.

Dear Heavenly Father,

Bless us to love one another regardless of our race, background, political party, and sexuality. We may not agree but let us show others that are lost and bound by the enemy, Your love so they can be converted, saved, and delivered. Place a love for others in our hearts. Thank you for answering this prayer in Jesus' name. Amen.

NO TERRORISM

1st John 4:20 (AKJ) says, "If a man says, I love God, and hateth his brother, he is a liar: for he that loveth not his brother whom he hath seen, cannot love God whom he hath not seen."

For many years, there have been conspiracies and lies circulating against African Americans and other races. There was a fear of their success and they were labeled as dangerous. However, it was groups such as the KKK that were really operating in hate. These groups were domestic terrorists because they lynched black people, burned down their houses, and killed because of racism. God is vindicating this injustice right now and many policies and laws to protect people are now in place. Before we talk about foreign terrorism and judge groups outside of the USA, we must first deal with our issues as a nation. All terrorism is wrong. We saw the devastation of September 11, 2001. However, no one should be afraid and terrorized because they are different.

Dear Heavenly Father,

Bless us to deal with the hard questions and bring healing to our land. You judge righteously and avenge us. Don't allow hate groups and terrorists to get away with evil. Bless them and save their souls from destruction. Keep Your people safe and out of harm's way. Thank You for answering this prayer in Jesus' name.

PEACEMAKERS

Matthew 5:9 (ESV) says, "Blessed are the peacemakers, for they shall be called sons of God."

When scandals happen, we must take charge and make peace. It's easy to fight and argue with each other. We need to demonstrate the power of God and be imitators of Christ. The enemy has his agents instigating situations and making things worse. However, Christians need to speak the truth and encourage those to make peace. There will always be disagreements. Yet, God will give us wisdom on how to handle our differences without fighting, bloodshed, or shame. Even when we disagree and want to protest, we need to do it peacefully. We witnessed looting in the COVID-19 pandemic, and that is wrong.

Dear Heavenly Father,

I pray that we can be peacemakers so You can get the Glory. I don't want to grieve Your Holy Spirit by operating in pride, rebellion, wrath, or malice. Lord, You warn us not to give into foolish controversies because they aren't fruitful and produce nothing good (2 Timothy 2:23). Bless Your people to get a hold of their flesh and yield to You in Jesus' name. Amen.

BROTHERLY LOVE

Hebrews 13:1 (ESV) says, "Let brotherly love continue."

God is love (1 John 4:7) and we commandment multiple times to love one another. If God says something repeatedly, then we must obey. Christians must be different and set the bar. This standard is based on the Word of God. How can we win people to God's Kingdom by being rude or nasty? Don't hurt your witness by not loving people. So many people are hurting and broken. They need a Savior, Jesus, who will set them free. However, their first encounter with Jesus will be through us because we are members of His Body (1 Corinthians 12:12). We are called to preach the Gospel to the ends of the Earth (Mark 16:15).

Dear Heavenly Father,

I declare that Your people will allow brotherly love to continue even if they feel hurt. Allow them to cast their cares upon You and You will sustain them (1 Peter 5:7). You have given us the ministry of reconciliation (2 Corinthians 5:18) and Your heart is to bring restoration. Bless us to love one another so You can be glorified. Thank You for answering this prayer in Jesus' name. Amen.

Appreciate each other's uniqueness

Mark 12:31 (NIV) says, "The second is this: 'Love your neighbor as yourself.' There is no commandment greater than these."

God has made each of us unique, and we all have something of value to bring to the table. Sometimes when people are unique, they are misunderstood. They then become a target of ridicule. We are God's handiwork (Ephesians 2:10). We must learn to work with others who may not sound or flow like us. During the Azusa Revival, God used a cock-eyed Black man named William Seymour to be the head of this movement. Some didn't want to receive God because they couldn't get past the racism in their hearts. Others didn't care and just wanted God. Don't reject the package your blessing comes in. We must respect each other and appreciate one another while we are in the land of the living.

Dear Heavenly Father,

I am not in control, but You are and know exactly what You are doing. You are sovereign and don't make mistakes. I will not reject my blessings or the package it comes in. If there is racism or insecurity in my heart, please remove it. I just want to walk in Your will and be pleasing in Your sight. Thanks for answering this prayer in Jesus' name. Amen.

UPROOT HATRED FROM OUR HEARTS

1 John 3:15 (ESV) says, "Everyone who hates his brother is a murderer, and you know that no murderer has eternal life abiding in him."

The spirit of hatred has been around for years. We see this spirit with Joshua and his brothers (Genesis 37:3-8). Also, we witness it in the story of Cain and Abel (Genesis 3). When someone is being blessed, we should rejoice. However, there is much competition and jealousy running rampant that prevents people from celebrating others. They are blinded by hate and can't see the change or the great work the individual might be doing. Dr. Martin Luther King Jr. was a peacemaker and fought for change. However, there was hatred in the President's heart that was in office and even the FBI during this time. They constantly spied on him and tried to destroy his reputation. Another example of hatred is Adolf Hitler's agenda to assassinate the Jews.

Dear Heavenly Father,

I can't make it into heaven hating others. Hatred is a work of the flesh and it's grievous to You. This spirit is against everything that You stand for Lord. Bless us to be delivered from hate and every evil work. I just want to bless You and allow you to get the glory out of my life. Thank You for answering this prayer in Jesus' name. Amen.

SALVATION

2 Corinthians 7:10 (NIV) says, "Godly sorrow brings repentance that leads to salvation and leaves no regret, but worldly sorrow brings death."

It is not God's will for anyone to perish. He desires all to be saved but some refuse Him and the message of salvation. Many lost people are operating in all spheres of the government, media, education, business, entertainment, arts, etc. They are bound by Satan and some don't recognize it. It's our job to be a light in dark places for them. If these people were truly saved, things would be better in our nation. We must focus on Jesus and develop a relationship with Him.

Dear Heavenly Father,

Lord, I pray that you send a godly sorrow that leads to repentance and salvation. You didn't create hell for mankind. It was created for Lucifer and the fallen angels. Bless people that we cross paths with to be open to receiving the message of the Gospel. Give us strategies and wisdom on how to witness effectively. Thank You for answering this prayer in Jesus' name. Amen.

HEALING IN OUR LAND

2 Chronicles 7:14 says, "If my people, which are called by my name, shall humble themselves, and pray, and seek my face, and turn from their wicked ways; then will I hear from heaven, and will forgive their sin, and will heal their land."

There are a lot of broken systems and people are suffering as a consequence. Daily we see strife and tension among our leaders. The crime rates are increasing and laws are becoming more wicked. The solution is Jesus. The system has been trying to eradicate Him for a long time and allow false deities in His place. When prayer was allowed in schools, there were no school shootings. Now school shootings have been common. Things have become bad and now some are crying out to God for help. We must repent as a nation and turn from our wicked ways. With prayer, God can uproot yokes of wickedness.

Dear Heavenly Father,

Thank you for being faithful. Please bring healing to our land and establish Your Word again. Protect our right to worship You. Overturn wicked decrees and attacks of the enemy. We repent, humble ourselves, turn from our wicked ways, and cry out to You for deliverance. Have mercy on us God and set us free. Thank You for answering this prayer in Jesus' name. Amen.

DELIVERANCE FROM PAIN, FEAR, WEARINESS, HURT, ETC.

Psalm 34:18 (ESV) says, "The Lord is near to the brokenhearted and saves the crushed in spirit."

Some people are so bound that they turn to drugs, alcohol, or sex to cope with their pain. They don't recognize that God can only fill the empty void in their hearts. We don't need prescriptions to mask the pain, fear, hurt, or depression. We need the power of God to heal all wounds. When God does a work, He does it completely. We must trust God for vindication.

Dear Heavenly Father,

Bless people to turn to You instead of running away when they go through trials in life. Allow them to surrender all and seek Your face. As they do, show them that you will deliver them from their pain, fear, weariness, hurt, etc. Allow them to trust and depend on You. Thank You for answering this prayer in Jesus' name. Amen.

God's Will

*G*OD'S WILL NEEDS TO be done in this nation because there is so much wickedness on the earth. We need to constantly cry out to God to bring Heaven down to Earth. It's time for God's people to get into position and take our stand against injustice. It's not the will of God for us to be sick, killed, poor, and bound. When God's glory manifests on the Earth, revival and spiritual awakening will happen.

God's kingdom to be established

Matthew 6:33 (ESV) says, "But seek first the kingdom of God and his righteousness, and all these things will be added to you."

God's Kingdom will not be shaken or destroyed. The enemy is constantly trying to come against it. Christians are being persecuted and demonic agendas seem to be on the rise. We must believe that we have the Kingdom of God inside of us. Once we know this fact, we can demonstrate God's power and authority in a greater measure. When God's Kingdom is established, there will be an outpouring of the Holy Spirit.

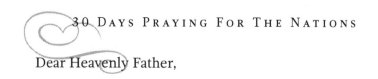

Dear Heavenly Father,

Bless Your Kingdom to be established. We bind up demonic attacks in the name of Jesus. Lord, strengthen Your people to cry aloud to spare not. Lord, uproot demonic strongholds and shake wickedness out of this earth. Lord, bring your glory down upon us. Thank You for answering this prayer in Jesus' name.

BELIEVERS TO HAVE INFLUENCE

Matthew 5:16 says, "In the same way, let your light shine before others, so that they may see your good works and give glory to your Father who is in heaven."

When you have influence on people, they listen to what you have to say. People will invest in your ideas, visions, business, and ministry. Many demonic people are in high positions of authority. They are doing things that are abominable in the Lord's sight. They have a form of godliness but denying the power thereof (2 Timothy 3:5). God has people who are walking uprightly before Him. They come to uproot and tear down demonic plots. Believers must reign on earth, so there can be an influx of souls.

Dear Heavenly Father,

You promote one and demote another. Give Your people influence in the different sectors of society. Lord, give your people influence to be a voice in important people's ears. Lord protect your people who are on the front lines from demonic attacks. Thank You for answering this prayer in Jesus' name. Amen

PURE MOTIVES

Matthew 5:8 (NKJV) says, "Blessed are the pure in heart, For they shall see God."

Believers need to have pure motives. Many people have motives. They want to be famous and rich while forgetting God in the process. Some start off right but then stumble. We must be fully submitted to God and yielded to Him because He knows what is best for our lives. If we obey Him, then we will receive His best. As we build a relationship with Him, we will get to know His heart and hear His voice. The glory of God will shine upon your life for others to see.

Dear Heavenly Father,

Bless me to have a pure heart so I can be pleasing in Your sight. Allow me to be a witness to the lost and demonstrate Your love without being judgmental. I pray that I can be trusted with their secrets and help them to be drawn to You as never before. Thank You for answering this prayer in Jesus' name. Amen.

NO SOUL LEFT BEHIND

Matthew 9:37-38 says, " Then saith he unto his disciples, The harvest truly is plenteous, but the labourers are few; Pray ye there-

fore the Lord of the harvest, that he will send forth labourers into his harvest."

It is not God's will for anyone to perish. We must care about the things that God is concerned about. Souls are one of them. Many are dying and going to hell daily. Are we telling others about Jesus? Sometimes the people that we cross paths with daily, like on our jobs, are our assignments. God is ordering our steps to plant seeds of the Gospel in their lives. If we don't witness unto them, then that blood will be upon our hands. The Gospel of the Lord Jesus Christ needs to proclaim on every corner. The church is Jesus' bride. Will we be ready when the bridegroom returns?

Dear Heavenly Father,

You are so worthy. You love sinners but hate the sin. I pray that we won't be so distracted or caught up in the cares of this world that we neglect You or run away from our purpose. Lord, may Your people consider Your ways so we can be about Your business and win souls. Bless us to be laborers in Your Kingdom. Thank You for answering this prayer in Jesus' name. Amen.

FOLLOW GOD'S COMMANDS

Isaiah 1:19 says, "If ye be willing and obedient, ye shall eat the good of the land:"

When we obey God's commands, the blessings will flow. People need to see the hand of the Lord upon our lives so they can want to serve Him as well. God will prosper His people in famine or a pandemic. He will make sure that our marriages and homes are blessed. We must obey God even when it's out of our comfort zone because He is stretching and taking us to another level. As we obey God and stay in His will, then we will be safe and covered. However, if we sin, the enemy can get it and cause chaos.

Dear Heavenly Father,

Lord, bless Your people to be sold out to You as we go out into the world. Strengthen our faith and bless us to pass every test. We want Your best for our lives and for Your plans to be fulfilled. Allow the sinner to desire a relationship with You when they see us living blessed, prosperous lives. Bless us to hide Your word in our hearts, so we don't sin against You.

Religious Freedom

IT APPEARS THAT THE days are growing more wicked and our religious freedom is underneath an attack. In certain nations, you are killed or arrested for preaching the Gospel. Some nations put restrictions on what a minister can preach, such as not preaching against homosexuality. Christians are censored on various social media platforms. Once I posted a Scripture about it's an abomination for a man to lie with another man and Facebook deleted my post. They said that I was posting hate and it went against their community standards. Shortly after, Facebook put some hindering algorithm on my public page and the exponential growth of followers and page likes slowed down drastically. Believers should have a right to post the Gospel without being censored on social media. God can raise up new platforms where our religious freedom isn't attacked. He can even allow policies to be changed. We must pray against the enemy trying to muzzle our mouths.

WON'T GET ARRESTED FOR PREACHING THE TRUTH
OF THE GOSPEL

John 17:17 says, "Sanctify them through thy truth: thy word is truth."

Many preachers worldwide have been arrested for preaching against sin.[14] There are laws in place that prevent preachers from sharing the whole gospel. As a result, horrible things are written about them on social media and they are charged with hefty fines. The enemy has an agenda and is trying his best to normalize sin. Believers shouldn't be afraid of man but fear God. Throughout Scripture, many of Jesus' disciples were arrested for preaching the gospel. Yet they didn't stop doing the work of their calling, neither should we.

Dear Heavenly Father,

Strengthen your servants who are preaching the message You gave them. Encourage them to stand strong in You and not shrink back. Protect them as they go forth. If they are arrested, bless funds to be available so they can make bail quickly. Anoint Your servants so more souls can be saved as they hear the truth of the Gospel. Amen.

LAWS TO BE PASSED THAT WON'T ATTACK RELIGIOUS FREEDOM

Galatians 5:1 (NASB) says, "It was for freedom that Christ set us free; therefore keep standing firm and do not be subject again to a yoke of slavery."

---

14. "Christian Preacher Arrested for Saying That Homosexual Behavior Is a Sin." n.d. Adflegal.org. Accessed May 10, 2021. https://adflegal.org/blog/christian-preacher-arrested-saying-homosexual-behavior-sin#close.

There are many gag orders to silence Christians from sharing their faith. Certain schools have passed policies where it is prohibited to pray or talk about Jesus. It is seen as taboo or offensive to specific groups if believers in Jesus preach in a public setting or outside the church. Years ago, the Johnson Amendment was put in place to prevent preachers from speaking out against certain political candidates. This amendment was demonic. As a result, there have been many wicked people who sat in high positions that passed policies, rules, laws, and regulations that were designed to silence Christians.

Dear Heavenly Father,

Raise up Your servants to be in position to vote against demonic agendas. Bless them with boldness so they can speak out against Satan's plans. Veto every law that goes against Your Word. Uproot every seed of the enemy. Thank You for answering this prayer in Jesus' name. Amen.

GODLY POLITICIANS/LEADERS WHO WILL STAND UP FOR THE CHURCH

Psalm 33:12 says, "Blessed is the nation whose God is the Lord; and the people whom he hath chosen for his own inheritance."

There are a few politicians that are open about their faith. Mike Pence and Ben Carson are two examples.[15] [16] They are called to be a light in dark places. They have to remain pure and be corrupted by the system because they are on assignment for God. The Lord is calling more of His servants to enter politics on all levels. Don't despise the instructions to get involved in the city council meetings or running for an office. The local and state level has power too. If God's people don't rise to fill these positions, then more agents of Satan will sit in these seats.

Dear Heavenly Father,

Thank You for sending Your people to sit in high places of authority. Protect them as they sound the alarm. Shield their hearts and minds from the attacks, especially negative publicly from the media. Allow them to draw closer to You to hear Your voice for guidance. Keep them pure so they will never compromise. Amen.

WON'T BE ACCUSED OF HATE CRIMES

1 John 3:10 says, "By this the children of God and the children of the devil are obvious: anyone who does not practice righteousness is not of God, nor the one who does not love his brother and sister."

---

15. DAntonio, Michael, and Peter Eisner. "As Donald Trump Faces Rising Dangers, 12 Religion Questions for Understudy Mike Pence." USA Today. September 13, 2018. Accessed July 06, 2021. https://www.usatoday.com/story/opinion/2018/09/13/mike-pence-christian-first-how-govern-president-donald-trump-column/1259832002/.
16. "Dr. Ben Carson - A Christian, First and Foremost." Ohio Christian University. July 07, 2020. Accessed July 06, 2021. https://www.ohiochristian.edu/news/advance-ment/dr-ben-carson-christian-first-foremost.

The enemy is busy spreading lies and twisting the truth of God's Word. God is love and He loves everyone. The enemy has brainwashed some people's minds to believe that Christians are full of hate and judgment because they support their sinful lifestyle. Just because you don't agree with sin doesn't mean you don't love others. Since people believe Satan's deceit, they accuse believers of Jesus of hate crimes and discrimination. Laws must be passed to protect our religious freedom. The right people must always fill governmental seats. If not, then someone who has no connection with God will pass laws contrary to our faith.

Dear Heavenly Father,

Keep your people strong as they are falsely accused for righteousness' sake. Remind us that we are blessed when we are persecuted. Allow us never to back down or quit when the enemy uses people to come against us when we preach Your word. I bind up the weariness off Your people. You will never leave us or forsake us in Jesus' name. Amen.

WON'T LOSE FUNDING OR TAX BENEFITS FOR PREACHING THE GOSPEL

1 Peter 4:16 (ESV) says, "Yet if anyone suffers as a Christian, let him not be ashamed, but let him glorify God in that name."

Many Christians are afraid of becoming incorporated or becoming tax-exempt because they don't want the government to control their ministry. They are also scared to preach certain messages because they don't want to lose their tax status. The government should not control how the church worships. God hasn't given us a spirit of fear. President Donald Trump signed laws into place to protect freedom of religion. However, we must not let our guards down and become complacent. We still have to intercede because another President might reverse this law. Christians must not fear man because it is a snare. We have to believe in God.

Dear Heavenly Father,

It is not Your will for Your children to struggle. When one door closes, You will open up another one. You are an excellent provider. We don't trust in the government but in You, God. It's a blessing not to pay taxes, but if we need to, then You will provide. Break off any fear and bondage from our lives. Thank You for guidance and insight in Jesus' name. Amen.

WON'T BE PERSECUTED/KILLED BECAUSE WE ARE CHRISTIANS

2 Corinthians 12:10 (ESV) says, "For the sake of Christ, then, I am content with weaknesses, insults, hardships, persecutions, and calamities. For when I am weak, then I am strong."

Persecution comes with the calling of God. Some of us don't want to go through anything. God warns us that if we desire to live a godly life, we will go through persecution. However, we are anointed for the attacks. The warfare is an indication that you are in the will of God. Christians need wisdom to navigate through the persecution. There were many martyred for the Gospel of Jesus. Stephen was stoned to death because he shared his faith (Acts 7:54-60). As believers, we don't have to be afraid of death because we have the gift of eternal life. One day, we will be with our Heavenly Father and enjoy eternal fellowship.

Dear Heavenly Father,

Prepare and equip Your people to fight the good fight of faith. Bless them not to get discouraged as they do Your will. Send angels to keep charge over them as they go out on the mission field. Give Your servants discernment so they won't succumb to the devil's attacks. Thank You for answering this prayer in Jesus' name. Amen.

RIGHT TO PRAY IN SCHOOLS/BUSINESSES

The Supreme Court has never outlawed praying in school.[17]However, there will always be someone who will oppose prayer in school. Some of these places have prohibited Christian groups but allowed other religions. Others have even banned the Bible. The First Amendment of the Constitution needs to be upheld. When prayer and the Bible were in the school system, school shootings were almost unheard of but now it's common. Every week on the news, there is another mass shooting. Boundaries need to be set in place where businesses have the right to practice their religious beliefs. There

17. "Is It Legal for Students to Pray in Public Schools? | Freedom Forum Institute." n.d. Accessed May 10, 2021. https://www.freedomforuminstitute.org/about/faq/is-it-legal-for-students-to-pray-in-public-schools/#:~:text=Contrary%20to%20popular%20myth%2C%20the.

have been many lawsuits against businesses because they didn't accept or service those who were living in a way contrary to their faith. For instance, Hobby Lobby, Chick-fil-a , and a few small Christian businesses were taken to court. Most of these cases were dismissed and God's people got the victory.

Dear Heavenly Father,

Thank You for giving Your people the victory each time they are threatened with lawsuits or accused of hate. Protect the school, businesses, and churches from vandalism or hate crimes when people get mad at our faith. Bless Your people to be bold and allow Your Word to go forth all over with power and demonstration. We bind up every demonic attack. Thank You for answering this prayer in Jesus' name. Amen.

Church

IF THE CHURCH GETS in position, a lot of what is occurring in the world wouldn't take place. It seems as the days are eviler and the enemy has penetrated several industries, platforms, and realms. The Body of Christ must no longer be silent or divided. We can't afford to be without power or demonstration. We must bring God's glory down to earth because His presence can shift atmospheres and soften hardened hearts.

PRAYING PEOPLE

1 Thessalonians 5:17 says, "Pray without ceasing."

Sadly, not a lot of church folks pray. They don't go to the prayer meetings and they are very carnal. They feel that five minutes of prayer a day is fine. Prayer is our opportunity to commune with God and to receive revelation from Him. It is through prayer that major moves of the Spirit happen and things turn around. If we want to see a change in our nation, then we must pray without ceasing. We need to have the mind of Christ on so we can pray to His will.

Dear Heavenly Father,

Give the church a burden for prayer and intercession. When there is a prayer meeting, allow Your people to attend and take it seriously. I bind up carnality and lethargy in the spirit. If Jesus prayed then, we must pray. Lord, teach us how to pray effectively in Jesus' name. Amen.

REVIVAL IN EVERY CITY

Psalm 85:6 says, "Will you not revive us again, that your people may rejoice in you?"

It would be wonderful if there were revivals in every city. The clubs would close. Crimes will stop. People will be on the streets crying out to God and repenting of their sins. These things may seem strange in our time, but there is nothing too hard for God. Throughout history, God has moved in cities and nations. As a result, there was a mighty harvest of souls. Revival is more than a fancy service for the church's program. It's about reviving the dead areas of our spiritual life and bringing it back into alignment with Jesus Christ. Revival is about the gathering of souls in the Body of Christ. Will you be a change agent and sacrifice so God can use you as a revivalist?

Dear Heavenly Father,

Send Your Glory fire to rain down upon our cities. Break off any traditions and allow us to yield to Your Spirit. Have Your way in our hearts and minds. Flow by Your power and demonstration so souls can be welcomed into Your Body. You know how to deal with us and set us free. Let signs, wonders, and miracles manifest on this Earth as never before. Thank You for answering this prayer in Jesus' name. Amen.

NO DEAD CHURCHES

Psalm 80:19 says, "Restore us, O Lord God of hosts! Let your face shine, that we may be saved!"

Many churches lack God's presence and they quench His Spirit. No one is getting saved, delivered, healed, or being transformed. People may have shouted and danced, but they can't remember what was taught. Some leave the same way that they came. As the Body of Christ, we need to be on fire for God. We should bring an anointing to the church and when we get together corporately, the presence of God should be strongly felt due to the corporate anointing. People need to see the gifts of the Spirit in operation because some won't believe God exists unless they have witnessed these things. Some churches aren't of God and practice abominable things, so they are void of God's presence. Will you allow God to have His way in you?

Dear Heavenly Father,

Allow the leaders or overseers of many churches to get back in right standing with You. Bless them to fast, pray, and allow You to have Your way in the service. Bless them to demonstrate your power as they did in the Book of Acts. Let these churches really be a place of refuge, healing, deliverance, and transformation to the lost and those working out their salvation. Thank You for answering this prayer in Jesus' name. Amen.

UNITY IN THE BODY REGARDLESS OF DENOMINATION

Psalm 133:1 (ESV) says, "Behold, how good and pleasant it is when brothers dwell in unity!"

The church is so divided that people fall out over the smallest issues. If people don't believe what you believe, they assume it's false or call things demonic when they don't understand something. For instance, some believe that the supernatural things of the Holy Spirit are for Charlatans. Others will call certain manifestations of God such as tongues, Holy Ghost fire, Word of Knowledge, or being slain in the spirit demonic. Martin Luther King Jr. said that Sunday morning was the most segregated hour in America. There are white, black, Korean, Hispanic, Asian, Baptist, Methodist, etc., churches. However, we all should have a common goal, Jesus. Also, we should love one another regardless of our differences.

Dear Heavenly Father,

Your Son Jesus prayed for His followers to be unified and to love one another. Bless your people to come together and work together. Allow them to be of a sound mind and spread the good news of the Lord Jesus Christ. Let love be the reason for everything. Thank You for answering this prayer in Jesus' name. Amen.

RESPECT FOR OTHERS

Romans 12:10 (ESV) says, "Love one another with brotherly affection. Outdo one another in showing honor."

People in the church need to respect each other. As soon as someone gets offended, they go on social media and attack the person they don't like. This method is out of order because they should come to the person in private. We have to be careful about speaking negatively about God's people. The Lord can judge us for coming against His friends. When the Sons of Korah came against Moses and Aaron, God opened up the earth and swallowed them (Numbers 16:32).

Dear Heavenly Father,

Bless your people to have respect for one another and demonstrate Your love. If they are offended, bless them to resolve the conflict in a way that is pleasing in Your sight. Deliver Your people from hurt and allow them to put their differences aside for Your glory. Thank You for answering this prayer in Jesus' name. Amen.

LEADERS WHO WILL NOT COMPROMISE

John 14:15 says, "If you love me, you will keep my commandments."

Many leaders have fallen into sin as a result of poor character. It hurts the Body of Christ when scandals emerge. Some are looking and vowing to never become a Christian due to the scandalous behavior of fallen ministers. Preachers have been involved in sexual immorality, prostitution, homosexuality, drugs, divination, child abuse, anger, etc. Leaders need to have a strong prayer life to resist temptation. Workers of iniquity will be evenly exposed. God is raising up pure vessels. Leaders need to be good stewards over the anointing that God has placed on their lives. Also, we need discernment and wisdom not to fall into the enemy's traps.

Dear Heavenly Father,

Bless Your servants to resist temptation and shun evil. Bless them not to grieve Your Spirit or bring shame unto You, Lord. I decree that they will be holy as You are holy. I pray that their hearts will be right in Your sight and that they will never sell out for money, fame, or opportunities. Thank You for answering this prayer in Jesus' name. Amen.

INFLUENCE.

Matthew 5:13 says, " Ye are the salt of the earth: but if the salt have lost his savour, wherewith shall it be salted? it is thenceforth good for nothing, but to be cast out, and to be trodden under foot of men."

The voice of the church needs to be heard. The enemy tries to silence the church so souls can stay in bondage and people won't be saved. The church can't stay silent on issues like abortion, gay marriage, economic crisis, pandemic, education, etc. We can't allow the enemy's threats to stop the church from speaking out and expressing the heart of God. God will raise up His servants with influence so that when they speak, people will listen.

Dear Heavenly Father,

Amplify Your servant's voices so people can hear Your heart and message. Bless them with boldness as they cry aloud and spare not. Protect them as they speak the truth and Your Word. Guide them in this world and open up doors for them to be heard. Thank You for answering this prayer in Jesus' name. Amen.

A LIGHT IN DARK PLACES

Matthew 5:14 says, "Ye are the light of the world. A city that is set on a hill cannot be hid."

The church must let the light of God's glory shine through them and become a beacon of light. Many people are lost and hurting. The church can help bring comfort, joy, strength, hope, and encouragement in trying times. We can't be afraid to share our faith, especially when we are at the workplace or in the community. Many souls need to be saved, so the church must get busy.

Dear Heavenly Father,

Bless Your people to be a light in dark places. Allow people to see the hands and feet of Jesus through us. Bless your church to be instruments of righteousness and allow You to flow. Allow us always to point people to Jesus and never themselves. Thank You for answering this prayer in Jesus' name. Amen.

GUIDANCE FROM THE LORD

Isaiah 30:21 says, "Whether you turn to the right or to the left, your ears will hear a voice behind you, saying, "This is the way; walk in it."

We need to allow God to guide us to be effective in our assignments. We have to put our agenda down and pick up the Lord's. There will be times when we want to preach a certain message, but the Lord will change it. God may even send us to certain ministries or churches for a select group of people who really need to hear what He has given us. When we allow God to guide us, we will be spared from danger. God will protect us.

Dear Heavenly Father,

Guide and order our steps. Allow us to be in the right place at the right time. Bless Your people with an ear to hear Your voice. Bless them with patience so they can wait on You. Bless them to trust Your plan and purpose for their lives. Thank You for answering this prayer in Jesus' name. Amen.

DEMONSTRATE THE POWER OF THE KINGDOM

1 Corinthians 2:4-5 says, "And my speech and my preaching was not with enticing words of man's wisdom, but in demonstration of the Spirit and of power: that your faith should not stand in the wisdom of men, but in the power of God."

Signs and wonders need to follow the church. In the Book of Acts, the supernatural was common and many people accepted Jesus in their hearts. When Jesus chose the twelve disciples, the number of followers quickly grew. They turned the world upside down. As we develop our relationship with Jesus, signs, wonders, and miracles will follow even when we aren't even trying. Also, we must preach the true Gospel of Jesus because signs and wonders follow the Word.

Dear Heavenly Father,

Let our preaching be demonstrated with Your power. Let blind eyes and deaf eyes be opened. Let the lame walk and the mute talk. Allow Your glory to saturate us as we yield to Your Spirit. Let the unbelievers accept Jesus into their hearts as we go forth in Your power. Thank You for answering this prayer in Jesus' name. Amen.

Economy

URING THE COVID-19 PANDEMIC, the economy crashed. Many people were out of work, homeless, hungry, and stressed out. The government had to issue several stimulus checks, loans, and tax breaks to help those impacted by the pandemic. Despite what was occurring, God prospered His people. Most were not even affected because the Lord is an excellent provider. The world needs to see the prosperity of the church so they will want to serve our God.

WEALTH FOR ALL SOCIAL CLASSES

Deuteronomy 8:18 says, "But thou shalt remember the Lord thy God: for it is he that giveth thee power to get wealth, that he may establish his covenant which he sware unto thy fathers, as it is this day."

There is a huge disparity between the rich and the poor. Certain laws enable the more affluent to write off their income to avoid paying taxes. Due to years of systemic racism, some ethnicities were hindered from accessing equal education, jobs,

homes, cars, etc. A lot of oppression surrounds them, so they have to work extra hard to get ahead in life.

Dear Heavenly Father,

Establish wealth for those who are overlooked in society. Some of Your people love You Lord but they are still broke. Allow them to be tested and tried, so You can trust them to have more in life. Reduce the wealth disparities in our nations and prosper Your servants. Thank You for answering this prayer in Jesus' name. Amen.

CURSES OF POVERTY ARE BROKEN

2 Corinthians 8:9 says, "For ye know the grace of our Lord Jesus Christ, that, though he was rich, yet for your sakes he became poor, that ye through his poverty might be rich."

People may come from nothing and never can get ahead in life due to several factors. However, God can increase them financially and sustain them. We can tithe and believe for a harvest because God promises to give seed to the sower. He also promises that when we give, it shall be given back to us. Jesus Christ is the curse breaker. Through Him, we can have wealth.

Dear Heavenly Father,

Break off generational curses off our bloodline. Prosper us with wealth and change our mindset when it comes to finances. I decree that we have been adopted into the bloodline of Jesus

Christ, who never lacked anything. I decree that our children's children will prosper and we will leave a legacy of wealth. Thank You for answering this prayer in Jesus' name. Amen.

GREAT STEWARDSHIP

1 Peter 4:10 (ESV) says, "As each has received a gift, use it to serve one another, as good stewards of God's varied grace."

We must be great stewards over our blessings and the things we take for granted. Some people inherited wealth and never had to work for anything. Others are not so fortunate and appreciate every opportunity afforded to them. If a person has a wrong mindset and is careless, they can lose everything, which is why some people win the lottery and blow that money quickly. We need wisdom and to be grateful for the things that God bestows upon our lives.

Dear Heavenly Father,

Bless us to be a great steward over our blessings. We never want to take things for granted. I decree that we have an attitude of gratitude. Lord, give us wisdom to guard what You gave us. I bind up carelessness and pride. I decree that we will never stumble and end up where we started from in Jesus' name. Amen.

LOVE GOD MORE THAN MONEY

Matthew 6:24 says, "No man can serve two masters: for either he will hate the one, and love the other; or else he will hold to the one, and despise the other. Ye cannot serve God and mammon."

God can't trust some with money because they will turn their backs on Him. They will seek God during the low moments in their lives. However, when things are going great, they forget God. Having a lot of money can kill some people because they have the opportunity to buy the harmful things they desire. For instance, if a crackhead has millions in the bank, they might blow it all on drugs and buy more crack than they can handle and potentially overdose. We must trust God and serve Him only, not the god of mammon.

Dear Heavenly Father,

Bless our hearts to be pure in Your sight. Bless us to love You with our whole heart, soul, and mind. Bless us to get Your Word in our hearts, so we don't sin against You. Bless us to fall deeper in love with You so we can keep Your commands. I decree that our motives will be right and we will not serve the god of mammon. Thanks for answering this prayer in Jesus' name. Amen.

SUPERNATURAL INHERITANCE

Proverbs 13:22 says, "A good man leaveth an inheritance to his children's children: and the wealth of the sinner is laid up for the just."

When we obey God, He will bless our children. There will also be a wealth transfer where the assets of the wicked are transferred to the righteous. God's children may suffer for a season but as they are faithful, God will increase their lives. God wants us to have financial security so we can be a blessing to others. When we can care for the less fortunate and do great works, God can be glorified. We need to believe God for strategies to eliminate debt so we can have more and do more.

Dear Heavenly Father,

Bless Your people to get out of financial bondage and allow them to prosper in life so they can leave an inheritance to their children. Allow them to pay off debt and give them strategies on how to do it. Establish them with financial security so they can focus on their godly assignments. Thank You for answering this prayer in Jesus' name. Amen.

Abundance

2 Corinthians 9:8 (NIV) says, "And God is able to bless you abundantly, so that in all things at all times, having all that you need, you will abound in every good work."

God desires for us to live an abundant life despite the economy. We are pilgrims here and passing through. We are in the world but not of the world. We are a lender and not a borrower. God will delight in our prosperity, increase, and abundance. We are above and never below. We are the head and not the tail. We are blessed in the city and country. Our vats are over-

flowing with new wine. As God causes our cups to overflow, we will have the financial security to bless others.

Dear Heavenly Father,

Thank You for always providing a ram in the bush for us. You anoint our heads with oil and our cups flow over. When You bless us, You go above and beyond anything that we can think or imagine. Allow sinners to be drawn to Jesus in us as they see the blessings in our lives. Bless us with opportunities to share of Your goodness. Thank You for answering this prayer in Jesus' name. Amen.

ASSETS ARE PROTECTED

Isaiah 32:18 (ESV) says, "My people will abide in a peaceful habitation, in secure dwellings, and in quiet resting places."

During the COVID-19 pandemic, many lost assets such as their homes, cars, stocks, or investments. The enemy's strategy is to divide and subtract. He comes to kill, steal, and destroy. However, God's plan is to increase and multiply. Jesus came to bring life much more abundantly. God can give us favor with the landlord, lender, or bank where they will work with us. He will make sure that we won't lose anything but gain. The ways of God are higher than ours. The natural mind can't comprehend the things of the spirit. God will supernaturally ensure that all our needs will be supplied. He will bless us with income, jobs, food, shelter, love, protection, comfort, and whatever we need.

Dear Heavenly Father,

Thank You Lord for Your provision and daily loading us with Your benefits. Thanks for the many blessings, favor, increase, abundance, wealth, protection, and other things that You have given me. We believe Your report. We will not be stressed out. You are Jehovah Jireh, our provider in Jesus' name. Amen.

DAY 10

Educators, Teachers, Students

OUR EDUCATORS AND STUDENTS need prayer. School shootings are common and the coronavirus is making people in school sick. Many teachers and students have died from COVID-19. The enemy is working overtime to force his agenda down our children's throats. We can't be silent on issues that arise. We must pray and take a stand so God's will can be done. God can bless them with wisdom and place His fear in their hearts. As the intercessors arise, the atmosphere can be peaceful and respectful. God can bring a mighty deliverance for those with disruptive behaviors. He will even turn the hearts of the parents to be on one accord with godly educators.

PROTECTION FROM VIRUS, MURDER, DESTRUCTION, AND BULLYING.

Psalm 91:10 (KJ21) says, "there shall no evil befall thee, neither shall any plague come nigh thy dwelling."

In 2020, America went on lockdown where schools and businesses closed due to a health crisis. Precautions were put in place, such as social distancing and wearing masks. Some schools opened up prematurely, and sadly some teachers and students became infected with COVID-19. There were measures put in place, such as spacing out desks, glass or plastic desk dividers, and ventilation systems. Some teachers quit because they didn't feel safe returning to work. Many schools defied government orders due to a lack of financial support to provide a safe environment for students. As a result, many schools transitioned to online. The pandemic has highlighted mental health issues. When some people get stressed, they want to hurt and kill others. God will keep us safe during any pandemic that we face. Our prayers will keep demonized people from killing our educators and children.

Dear Heavenly Father,

Protect teachers, educators, students, and anyone else that is a part of the educational system. Guide them on whether or not they should get vaccinated against the coronavirus. Bless those that are sick to recover and to stay home so others will not get sick. Send angelic forces to stand at the doorposts of the building to keep terrorists and murderers away. We bind up bullying and declare that the school house will be a peaceful environment. Thank You for answering this prayer in Jesus' name.

ADJUSTING TO THE NEW NORMAL

Numbers 23:19 (ESV) says, " God is not man, that he should lie, or a son of man, that he should change his mind. Has he said, and will he not do it? Or has he spoken, and will he not fulfill it?"

The 2020 pandemic has taught us a new way of doing life. We had to readjust to cope and to succeed in business and education. Children who couldn't have a prom or graduation put something together online. Schools had to adjust to smaller in-person class sizes or rotate different shifts for the students on different days. The biggest challenge was for students to wear a mask for up to eight hours a day. God can give us peace that surpasses all understanding in difficult times. He will also strengthen us and give us hope.

Dear Heavenly Father,

Give your people strength as they face new things. For those that don't know You, draw them to You. Allow them to hear your gospel and turn their hearts to You. Bless them to depend on You and bless them not to have a mental breakdown. I bind up stress and anxiety. Give Your people wisdom in Jesus' name. Amen.

GODLY CURRICULUM

Deuteronomy 4:9 (BSB) says, "Only be on your guard and diligently watch yourselves, so that you do not forget the things your eyes have seen, and so that they do not slip from your heart as long as you live. Teach them to your children and grandchildren."

Our children are the next generation and sadly most parents don't teach their children many things. They are taught life and social skills from their teachers. However, some educators go against things that are contrary to our faith. Some may teach children LGBTQ+ history, Halloween, or things that grieve the Holy Spirit. Demonic curriculums need to be exposed and parents need to stand up for their beliefs. If they have to home-school or choose another school that is aligned with their faith, they should be able to do so without retaliation from the education board. Parents should be involved in their children's education to make sure they grow up to be successful.

Dear Heavenly Father,

Expose evil curriculums and loose boldness upon every parent and educator. Allow educators to refuse to teach it and bless parents to stand up for righteousness. Bless the children with discernment and to walk uprightly before you. Touch the lawmakers so they can pass laws that will benefit our children and not harm them. Allow your truth to be revealed, God. I bind up every lie the devil is trying to spread in the education system in Jesus' name.

CHILDREN TO EXCEL

Daniel 6:3 (ESV) says, "Then this Daniel became distinguished above all the other presidents and satraps, because an excellent spirit was in him. And the king planned to set him over the whole kingdom."

Our children are the next generation and they are like sponges. They absorb and imitate the things they see adults do. When a child displays bad behavior, most likely they learned it at home. Parents will have to give an account for how they raise their children. There are discriminatory laws in place that hinder children from low income families or minorities from receiving an equal education. There should be a fair chance for these children and they should have access to the tools and re-sources and opportunities to do well in life. Our prayers can bring much needed funding, repairs, and improvement in tech-nology. God will cause supernatural things to happen so every child can have Wi-Fi access.

Dear Heavenly Father,

Uproot every discriminatory law that hinders our children. Expose any disparity in the education system. Lord, bless the school system with the funds they need so children can have new textbooks, computers, and a nice learning environment. Bless the children to excel on their exams and state testing. Al-low them to retain the information being taught so they can go to the next level. Thank you for answering this prayer in Jesus' name. Amen.

NO PEDOPHILES, RAPE, OR DANGER

Psalms 34:7 (NIV) says, "The angel of the Lord encamps around those who fear him, and he delivers them. "

Many scandals have occurred when the teachers have slept with their students or inappropriate behavior was exposed. There must be self-control so the flesh doesn't dominate us. Teachers must have moral standards and follow the school's protocols. Pedophiles shouldn't be allowed in the education system because many children will be prey. Some children are just as guilty. A crush on their instructor may evolve into something more. There are consequences that will occur if the line is crossed between teacher and student. As we pray, God will reveal any inappropriate relationships in our children's lives and those who are connected to them.

Dear Heavenly Father,

Protect our children from pedophiles. Bless each school to do background checks and put monitoring systems in place. Allow all parties to have accountability partners to give them sound counsel to not fall into sin. We bind up the enemy from lusting after our children. Lord, protect our children's innocence. Deliver our children who are on the wrong path. Thank you for answering this prayer in Jesus' name. Amen.

God's Protection

GOD IS SERIOUS ABOUT protecting his children. He promises that no hairs on our head will be touched. God will avenge us when we are wronged. He will even assign angels to protect us from destruction.

NO TERRORISM

2 Thessalonians 3:3 (NIV) says, "But the Lord is faithful, and he will strengthen you and protect you from the evil one."

There are many forms of terrorism. We know about international terrorism that occurred on September 11, 2001. A few airplanes were hijacked and crashed into the Twin Towers in New York. Then there is domestic terrorism, where hate groups arise. They will target people based on their skin color or beliefs. As we pray, we will overcome fear, insanity, and evil plots. Terrorism is a threat to national security. God will warn us of any danger so we can be still and avoid the enemy's plans.

Dear Heavenly Father,

Expose these hate groups and turn their hearts. Bless them to come out of darkness and into the light. Allow those who are considering joining these groups to turn away. Show these people the truth and open up their eyes so they can see how deceived they are so they won't die and go to hell. You warn us that if we are full of hatred, then we won't make it into your Kingdom in Jesus' name. Amen.

NO PLAGUES OR DISEASES

Isaiah 54:17 (NIV) says, "No weapon forged against you will prevail, and you will refute every tongue that accuses you. This is the heritage of the servants of the Lord, and this is their vindication from me," declares the Lord."

There are many diseases, but God promises that no plague shall come near our dwelling. The weapon may form, but it will not prosper. Many people are dying from Covid-19, the flu, strokes, and cancer. Jesus is a healer and He gives us the wisdom to make better lifestyle changes so we can take care of His temple or our bodies. We have work to do for the Lord and we can't be hindered by sickness.

Dear Heavenly Father,

Keep us safe and don't allow any emerging diseases to take us out. Cover us in the blood of Jesus. Bless us to build up our immune system, exercise, and eat healthy so we can have the strength to fight off any virus. Bless us to take heed to any precaution and follow the guidelines of those in authority so we

can be shielded from sickness. Thank you for answering this prayer in Jesus' name.

FOOD BORNE ILLNESS AND FOOD RECALLS

2 Timothy 4:18 (NIV) says, "The Lord will rescue me from every evil attack and will bring me safely to his heavenly kingdom. To him be glory for ever and ever. Amen."

Food recalls are becoming more common. There have been E. Coli outbreaks. Glass, plastic, and foreign objects are found in our packaged foods. Some of these recalls result from poor regulation of the food industry, poor work environments, and sick workers. God can warn us in prayer to avoid certain foods because He knows that there is danger ahead. We must obey Him and be willing to sacrifice our taste buds to Him.

Dear Heavenly Father,

Bless the foods that we consume. If there are any cancerous agents, remove them supernaturally. If any bacteria present will make us sick, sanctify the food before we consume it. Lord, bless higher safety standards to be implemented in our food supply. Order our steps to the right market or store so we can purchase food that isn't contaminated. Thank you for answering this prayer in Jesus' name. Amen.

SAFE TRANSPORTATION

Proverbs 18:10 says, "The name of the Lord is a fortified tower; the righteous run to it and are safe."

Many people have been attacked using public transportation like airplanes, trains, buses, or car rides. Some people prey on innocent people to rob or harm them. Sadly some people get caught in the crossfire. Many workers in the transportation industry have lost their lives and were injured on the job due to unruly and sick passengers. God can protect us from harm as we do our jobs or use public transportation.

Dear Heavenly Father,

Lord protect us as we board taxis, Ubers, Lyfts, buses, planes, trains, ships, or any other transportation. Please keep us from unseen harm and danger. Bless us to be in sync with Your Spirit so we can be at the right place at the right time. Lord, cause divine delays if there is a malfunction somewhere or impending danger. Don't allow our feet to enter into anything unsafe. Thank You for answering this prayer in Jesus' name. Amen.

SAFE WHILE SHOPPING, WORKING, OR ATTENDING WORSHIP SERVICES

Psalm 121:7-8 (NIV) says, "7 The Lord will keep you from all harm- he will watch over your life; 8 the Lord will watch over your coming and going both now and forevermore."

Every day we need to pray for God to protect us. Someone can come into the church or our workplace to shoot it up. God is merciful and He warns us in dreams, visions, or speaking to us. God will make a way of escape so we can walk away without a scratch. Unfortunately, violent crimes are on the rise and we don't need to be in the midst of it. Our prayers will keep the enemy away.

Dear Heavenly Father,

Bless us to stay off the path of destruction. If someone is planning to shoot up a building, prevent them from doing so because we are there. Allow their guns and weapons to malfunction if they try to use them. Lord, give these people who are planning evil a dream or warning so they won't hurt or kill anyone. Bless them to repent, get saved, and stop their evil works. Thank you for answering this prayer in Jesus' name.

NO CHEMICAL, BIOLOGICAL, OR NUCLEAR WARFARE

Psalm 32:7 (NIV) says, "You are my hiding place; you will protect me from trouble and surround me with songs of deliverance."

Many people became sick due to unsafe environmental practices. For example, some people live next to a factory where toxic waste enters the water supply or harmful gas is emitted into the atmosphere. Cancer or other ailments is a common thing in a certain community. Some impoverished communities tolerate this because they don't have the money to move. God can raise people up to change laws or prevent these corporations from doing unsafe practices.

Dear Heavenly Father,

We lift up big corporations who are negligent and caus-ing harm to the environment and people. Allow them to have compassion and stop their greedy ways so no more people will become sick. Allow these harmful corporations to relocate so they won't be around subdivisions, schools, or fragile wildlife. Thank you for answering this prayer in Jesus' name. Amen.

NO ROBBERIES

Nahum 1:7 (NIV) says, "The Lord is good, a refuge in times of trouble. He cares for those who trust in him."

God commands in His Word that we shall not steal. If the world followed God's commandments, it would be a better place. Unfortunately, some people covet what you have and don't want to work hard for it, so they will try to take your blessing. God can lead us, so we never become prey to rob-bery. He can cover our homes and vehicles with His glory so the enemy will never touch us. God can give us financial break-throughs to afford security systems and protect what He has given us.

Dear Heavenly Father,

Bless us to stay alert and be discerning so we will not be-come a victim to the enemy. He comes to kill, steal, and de-stroy. However, Jesus came to give life and life more abundant-ly. Lord, amp up security in our neighbors and communities so our homes, businesses, or churches will never get vandalized. Thank you for answering this prayer in Jesus' name. Amen.

NO FIRES, SAFE FROM NATURAL DISASTERS, AND SINKHOLES

Psalm 3: 3 (NIV) says, "But you, Lord, are a shield around me, my glory, the One who lifts my head high."

Every year in certain regions there are wildfires and many have to evacuate. There are sinkholes due to the limestone in the ground being eroded by moisture. Houses and cars are swallowed up, never to be recovered. Storms, tornados, floods, or hurricanes have taken many lives. Some lose everything and it takes them years to get back on their feet. God can sustain them and provide all their needs. God can bless us to overcome and spare us during these natural disasters.

Dear Heavenly Father,

Protect us from natural disasters. Bless the insurance companies to pay us anything that is owed if our homes have been destroyed. Give us wisdom when it comes to buying land and property so we will never be displaced. I bind up homelessness and lack in the name of Jesus. Thank You for answering this prayer in Jesus' name. Amen.

PROTECTING ALL FRONTLINE WORKERS, HEALTH-CARE, TRUCKERS, GROCERY STORE, FIREFIGHTERS, POLICEMEN

Deuteronomy 31:6 (NIV) says, "Be strong and courageous. Do not be afraid or terrified because of them, for the LORD your God goes with you; he will never leave you nor forsake you."

These workers are considered frontline because they have put their lives on the line during the COVID-19 pandemic and the civil unrest. They have been targeted with hate crimes and became sick from the virus doing their jobs. Yet, they had kept the country running when the government ordered a lockdown in 2020. We must keep these workers in prayers as they work because they have families and people who love them.

Dear Heavenly Father,

Give these workers peace and courage as they do their jobs. We bind up fear and mental health issues off their lives. Allow these people to trust You and have a relationship with you. Put a hedge of protection around them in Jesus' name. Amen.

Media

*T*HE MEDIA IS HOW we found out what is going on in the world. When an event, tragedy, or something new emerges, the media then reports this information on their platforms or on social media. However, some sources will twist the truth because they have an agenda. Sadly, some Christian networks have been caught up in political schemes when our main focus should be Jesus and soul winning. God will expose every lie as the truth is revealed.

TRUTH

John 8:32 (ESV) says, "And you will know the truth, and the truth will set you free."

God is truth and the enemy is the father of all lies. There is a demonic agenda in the media. Some people with the biggest platforms or who have many followers spread lies and conspiracies. We need discernment to cut through the false news. We can't have itching ears. If God shows us who has an ulterior motive, we need to cut that out of our lives, so we don't become deceived.

Dear Heavenly Father,

Expose every lie in the media and unravel every demonic agenda. Whatever is done in darkness will come to the light. Darkness will not overpower the light. Bless your people not to be caught up in gossip, hearsay, strife, malice, or evil works because it grieves Your Spirit. Lord, raise up pure media outlets that aren't influenced by the enemy. Thank You for answering this prayer in Jesus' name.

INTEGRITY

Proverbs 12:22 (ESV) says, "Lying lips are an abomination to the Lord, but those who act faithfully are his delight."

God is opening up doors for those who are after His heart to have their own shows, networks, or influence. These people will promote righteousness and shun evil. They will not waiver in the faith and get caught up in demonic trends. They will seek God in everything they report so He can get glorified. God will demote some and promote His people. These people and networks will purge out works of darkness and workers of iniquity. These networks will promote peace, and not stir up division or hatred. God will give these networks witty ideas to create programs, books, and resources that glorify Him.

Dear Heavenly Father,

Raise up more media outlets that will give You the glory. It is not Your will for the enemy to dominate the media industry. You desire to have the media industry to be used as a powerful evangelist tool to win souls. Bless Your people to not be afraid of social media. Enlightened them with the benefits of being on social media in Jesus' name. Amen.

PURITY

Psalm 25:5 (ESV) says, "Lead me in your truth and teach me, for you are the God of my salvation; for you I wait all the day long."

The enemy is using the media to spread his lies and plots. We must be on high alert and sound the alarms so we don't become prey. The enemy targets the youth because he knows they are the next generation. If he can win them over while they are young, he can steer their lives. Our children to be protected from evil agendas. There isn't much wholesome content available because there are vulgar language, sexual scenes, repulsive acts, and demonic plots that grieve the Holy Spirit. Also, there seems to be more bad news that draws a lot of attention than good news. Some people love feeding their spirits with bad news. God will convict those outside of His will. He will even raise up news outlets to give us hope, encouragement, healing, inspiration, and godly instructions.

Dear Heavenly Father,

Let the media outlet be a tool for righteousness. Allow the Holy Spirit to convict those outside of God's will. I decree the media will be a powerful tool for God instead of the enemy. I decree that the media will influence godliness instead of evil. Thank You for answering this prayer in Jesus' name. Amen.

Other Nations

*P*ALM 33:12 (ESV) SAYS, *"Blessed is the nation whose God is the Lord, the people whom he has chosen as his heritage!"*

We need to pray for other nations because some are suffering from things that Americans aren't on a massive scale. Americans have a right to education, access to technology, and better healthcare. Other nations may not have this luxury. God can provide all of their needs and be glorified.

PROTECT AMBASSADORS AND MISSIONARY OVERSEAS

Matthew 24:14 (ESV) says, "And this gospel of the kingdom will be proclaimed throughout the whole world as a testimony to all nations, and then the end will come."

Our workers need to be protected as they go into some of these countries. Some nations hate Americans and Christians. The Bible is even banned and they will kill for their beliefs. God will shield them from harm. If they are arrested, God can make a way of escape. The church must pray for the nation's deliverance.

Dear Heavenly Father,

Shield our government and your people from acts of terrorism. We bind up hatred and every evil work in Jesus' name. Strengthen Your people overseas so they will not lose faith and hope in You. Give them courage and remind them that You are with them and will never leave them. Thank You for answering this prayer in Jesus' name. Amen.

SERVICE AND LAW ENFORCEMENT AGENCIES TO WORK TOGETHER

Isaiah 2:4 (ESV) says, "He shall judge between the nations, and shall decide disputes for many peoples; and they shall beat their swords into plowshares, and their spears into pruning hooks; nation shall not lift up sword against nation, neither shall they learn war anymore."

Some nations allow the mafia, gangs, warlords to run rampant because they depend on them for protection. Some law enforcement are on their payroll and don't work with outside officials due to the high corruption. The people are suffering and flee the country for the hopes of a better life. God can uproot every demonic scheme and bring reformation to a hurting nation. God can remove wicked governments and raise up godly leadership. God can put an end to senseless murders and corruptions as the church prays.

Dear Heavenly Father,

You are so worthy. Allow the hidden schemes to be exposed. Bless the people who walk uprightly before You as they stand against unrighteousness. Allow the corrupt leaders to turn from their wicked ways, repent, and develop a relationship with You. Bless them not to be brought. Protect them from any threats in Jesus' name. Amen.

NO HUMAN TRAFFICKING

Psalm 22:28 (ESV) says, "For kingship belongs to the Lord, and he rules over the nations."

The sex industry is huge in some nations. Some children are kidnapped or sold to generate wealth. The victims are caught into a system that they want to get out of but they don't know what to do. As a result, they become abusers and do to others what was done unto them. God will send brave people into these regions to bring change and to spread the Gospel. God can end human trafficking and expose every evil work.

Dear Heavenly Father,

Send angelic forces to protect innocent people from being a prey of human trafficking. Allow families to stick together and put measures of security in place to protect themselves from the adversary. For those who are caught up in the system, provide a way of escape. Bless those in authority to get involved and shut down every demonic work. Thank You for answering this prayer in Jesus' name. Amen.

GENOCIDE

2 Chronicles 7:14 (ESV) says, "If my people who are called by my name humble themselves, and pray and seek my face and turn from their wicked ways, then I will hear from heaven and will forgive their sin and heal their land."

Certain nations are killing each other for land, tribal beliefs, sex, greed, gender, and religion. Some groups rise up and acquire weapons so they can overthrow the government. It's a chaotic environment and war among the people. Sometimes the United States has to get involved to bring order so these militia groups don't kill any more innocent victims. Our prayers can bring peace and harmony to a nation that is crying out over spilled blood.

Dear Heavenly Father,

Bring an end to genocide and evil work in the nations whose land is crying out. Allow these people to turn to You so they can get the freedom that Jesus died for on the cross. Bless the people in these nations to be peacemakers and to live peaceably with all. Allow them to put their differences aside and work together so You can be glorified. Thank You for answering this prayer in Jesus' name. Amen.

SUPPLIES, FOOD, CLOTHES, AND REFUGE

Philippians 4:19 says, "But my God shall supply all your need according to his riches in glory by Christ Jesus."

Many nations are poor and lack essential supplies to get a proper education. They lack food, clothes, and shelter. Some children are skin and bones. They are dying from starvation. Some people eat dirt, grass, bugs, and drink dirty water that is making them sick. Reformation and access to clean water is needed. These nations have a health crisis because in the same water supply they cook and drink with, someone is urinating and taking a bath. Some people have to walk miles to get water. God can send people in these nations to dig wells and do humanitarian acts.

Dear Heavenly Father,

You are the God who supplies all of our needs. You work miracles and cause supernatural things to happen. Bless the hungry to have food. Bless the thirsty to have access to clean water. Bless the naked to have clothes. Bless the poor to have money to take care of their families. Thank You for answering this prayer in Jesus' name. Amen.

RAISE UP GODLY LEADERS

Psalm 22:27 (ESV) says "All the ends of the earth shall remember and turn to the Lord, and all the families of the nations shall worship before you."

God will send His people into uncharted territories to spread the good news of the gospel. He will pour out His Spirit and cause a spiritual awakening. A harvest is waiting to come into the Kingdom as the Gospel is preached. God will even cause a revival for those who need a fresh touch of His Spirit. God has sent many people into nations to plant churches and appoint capable men to oversee them. As God moves into these nations, they will serve Jesus, renounce idolatry and get delivered from false religion.

Dear Heavenly Father,

Have Your way in the nations. Draw people to You and show Yourself strong and mighty. Let those who never heard Your message, hear it for the first time. Let Your power flow so people can be saved and set free. Let churches be planted and increase in number. Thank You for answering this prayer in Jesus' name. Amen.

HEALTH AND ACCESS TO VACCINATIONS/ HEALTHCARE

Proverbs 14:34 (ESV) says, "Righteousness exalts a nation, but sin is a reproach to any people."

During the COVID-19 pandemic certain nations were highlighted as they lacked access to healthcare. Some countries couldn't vaccinate their people so the virus spread, killing many. Other nations have outbreaks of polio, measles, or other diseases that Americans have been vaccinated against. As a

result, some people in these countries seek Shamans or witch doctors for their healing. They need to know that God heals and it is His will for them to be in good health.

Dear Heavenly Father,

Allow the impoverished nations to have access to health-care. Upgrade the technology in these countries and allow them to receive top notch care. Allow them to seek You instead of a false deity. Send resources, medicine, and supplies into these nations so You can get the glory. Thank You for answering this prayer in Jesus' name. Amen.

Healing

*T*HERE IS SO MUCH healing that needs to take place in our nation. The COVID-19 has highlighted various issues and wounds began to surface. One thing for sure is that the nation is in need of a Savior. God can bring the unity that is needed so we can move forward as He rights the wrongs and exposes wickedness.

AN EFFECTIVE VACCINE FOR COVID

Jeremiah 8:22 (ESV) says, "Is there no balm in Gilead? Is there no physician there? Why then has the health of the daughter of my people not been restored?"

In 2020, scientists from all over the world worked hard to develop a vaccine for COVID-19. Many were skeptical because the vaccines were developed so quickly. Some cases arose where there were adverse reactions such as blood clots, swelling, and convulsions. However, President Biden, celebrities, and the media have worked hard to convince Americans that the vaccine was safe, but some refuse to take it. The vaccines can have a higher efficiency rate even though they provide 70 to 90 percent protection.

Dear Heavenly Father,

Take You for technology and advancement in medicine to save lives. Lead and guide us on whether or not we should get vaccinated. If the vaccine will cause severe reactions, bless us to avoid receiving a bad batch. Increase the efficiency rate, so no one gets reinfected with Covid or dies from it. Thank You for answering this prayer in Jesus' name. Amen.

HEALING IN OUR EMOTIONS

Job 5:18 (ESV) says, "For he wounds, but he binds up; he shatters, but his hands heal."

There has been a rise of mental health crises because people are stressed due to the pandemic, economic strain, and civil unrest. People are committing suicide to end it all. Suicide is not the best way because their actions affect their loved ones. God can set us free with His power. As a result, we can have peace that surpasses all understanding.

Dear Heavenly Father,

Thank You for sending Your only begotten Son Jesus to die on the cross for our sins. Who the Son sets free is free indeed. Allow us to get a handle on our emotions during this time. Allow us to trust You with everything within us. Thank You for answering this prayer in Jesus' name. Amen.

HEALING FROM PAST EVENTS

Jeremiah 30:17 (ESV) says, "For I will restore health to you, and your wounds I will heal, declares the Lord, because they have called you an outcast: 'It is Zion, for whom no one cares!'"

America has an ugly history. Men came from Europe and killed a bunch of Native Americans for their land. Then they brought slaves from Africa. These slaves made their masters very rich off their labor. A lot of injustice occurred and false promises were made. Jim Crow laws were passed that made things worse. Congress has been talking about providing reparations for the ancestors of slaves as a tool for healing past wounds.

Dear Heavenly Father,

Bless this nation to rebuild and move forward despite our past. Recompense us and shake out wickedness from the earth. We can't change history, but we can admit our wrongs and learn from our mistakes. Lord, bridge the gap and close the racial divide. Level the playing field. Thank You for answering this prayer in Jesus' name. Amen.

Health Care

*H*EALTH CARE HAS BEEN a big topic for many years. Many people in America are uninsured because they can't afford the high price of insurance. Some of the people in the industry don't care about saving lives but are only concerned with making money. Many have got into severe debt because of medical bills. American healthcare needs to be reformed. Our prayers can make it happen.

AFFORDABLE HEALTHCARE

3 John 1:2 (ESV) says, " Beloved, I pray that all may go well with you and that you may be in good health, as it goes well with your soul."

President Obama passed the affordable care act where it was mandatory for people to get insurance or they would be fined when they filed their taxes. The insurance companies were supposed to have lower premiums, but that wasn't always the case. New laws are in place where consumers can now see the cost for everything or a more detailed bill to help them understand the charges for medical services. Certain communities don't even have access to quality care. Our prayers can shift things for the underserved and overlooked.

Dear Heavenly Father,

Thank You for Your healing power and answering our prayers. You see the greed and injustice in our healthcare system. Give us the wisdom to make the system effective so people can get the help that they need. Allow universal healthcare to be put in place so everyone can have access to quality health care in Jesus' name. Amen.

EXPOSE AND CORRECT CORRUPTED INSURANCE COMPANIES

Ephesians 5:11 (ESV) says, "Take no part in the unfruitful works of darkness, but instead expose them."

Some insurance companies don't want to pay out or compensate to whom money is owed. As a result, many healthy individuals are paying high premiums and they rarely go to the doctor. Sometimes the insurance company refuses to pay for services, so the healthcare provider has to now go after the consumer to get paid. Also, some of these insurance companies deny those with pre-existing conditions so they don't have to spend a lot of money on them or their care.

Dear Heavenly Father

Crack down on injustice and those who take advantage of the healthcare system. Allow these companies to keep their word and not exploit those who need help. Allow your people who need help to receive the care that they need without dealing with the stress of a wicked company. Thank You for answering this prayer in Jesus' name. Amen.

INCREASE MEDICAL ADVANCEMENTS/TECHNOLOGY TO IMPROVE CARE

Exodus 23:25 (ESV) says, "You shall serve the Lord your God, and he will bless your bread and your water, and I will take sickness away from among you."

Some facilities have funds and enough equipment to save lives without turning those in need away. Their workers are skilled and provide the best care possible. However, the COVID-19 pandemic exposes a lot of strains on the healthcare system. Many facilities didn't have enough protective equipment such as masks, face shields, gowns, or gloves. As a result, many of their staff became infected with the coronavirus and some died. Also, there was a shortage of ventilators and oxygen, so many companies stepped up and produced what was needed.

Dear Heavenly Father,

Improve the level of care that we receive. Allow each facility that we visit to have adequate staff and top notch equipment. Bless the facility to be clean to prevent any infections that will try to attach itself to us. Bless each facility to review the current medical research so they will not use outdated practices in Jesus' name. Amen.

PEACE FOR HEALTHCARE WORKERS

2 Thessalonians 3:16 (ESV) says, "Now may the Lord of peace himself give you peace at all times in every way. The Lord be with you all."

Working in healthcare can be fast paced and stressful. When a lot is going on, some people snap or have a horrible attitude. God can give them peace as they seek Him. They need to trust Him for their protection and well being. These workers need to have empathy, patience, and strength as they work so they can provide the best care.

Dear Heavenly Father,

Protect the healthcare workers, especially when new viruses emerge. Give them peace, strength, and hope. Allow them to trust in You during stressful times. Bless them to be optimistic and encourage their patients and co-workers. Thank You for answering this prayer in Jesus' name. Amen.

PHARMACY

Matthew 9:12 (ESV) says, "But when he heard it, he said, "Those who are well have no need of a physician, but those who are sick."

Some people can't afford the high cost of medicine, so they die prematurely. There are third parties involved and they make money off medicine. Many don't care about saving lives but care more about their pockets. They get their drugs patent and can raise the price of their drugs. These drugs are life and death. For that reason, certain drugs like insulin must stay low in price, so laws have been passed to protect people with diabetes. Many Americans have gone to other countries to get drugs that were a fraction of the cost. Yet, corrupt individuals put laws in place to hinder people from doing this, knowing that some are desperate to live due to being terminal. Greed is the culprit. These wicked individuals want as much money as possible. Some are even lobbying and influencing Congress to pass laws in their favor even though it will hurt the average person.

Dear Heavenly Father,

Bless us to get any medicine that we need without going broke or getting into debt. Prevent life saving drugs from being exploited or out of reach for those who truly need them. Allow people to have a choice on the drugs they buy for their care without having laws that restrict them from receiving options. We pray that there will be no political agenda. Thank You for answering this prayer in Jesus' name. Amen.

Voter Suppression

THROUGHOUT HISTORY, THERE HAS been voter suppression. Some white supremacist groups and racist lawmakers used fear tactics and even lynched black people from voting. Now, they put fewer polls in predominantly black areas. Lawmakers pass all kinds of laws to make voting hard so people can get discouraged and not vote. These methods have been exposed and many groups and businesses have boycotted. In March 2021, a few Georgian lawmakers passed such laws.[18]

BELIEVERS TO VOTE AND SERVE AT THE POLLS

Psalm 9:9 (ESV) says, "The Lord is a stronghold for the oppressed, a stronghold in times of trouble."

Christians are known for their integrity because they are imitators of Jesus. If there was ever a problem in the voting systems, Christians can be trusted to be honest so there will be no voter fraud. Even during the 2020 election, there were

18. Corasaniti, Nick. 2021. "Georgia G.O.P. Passes Major Law to Limit Voting amid Nationwide Push." The New York Times, March 25, 2021, sec. U.S. https://www. nytimes.com/2021/03/25/us/politics/georgia-voting-law-republicans.html.

lies floating around of fraud, there were appointed witnesses to watch the recounts. Some believers don't want to get involved in politics, but it matters who sits in power or governs because their laws affect us. No one should be discriminated against because of race, sex, political party, or age.

Dear Heavenly Father,

Order our steps and allow us to vote for the right person. If there is an opportunity to serve at the polls, bless us to do so. Open up doors that no man can shut. Bless us to stand up for righteousness and cry out against injustice. Expose every lie and let the truth be revealed. Thank You for answering this prayer in Jesus' name. Amen.

NO DISCRIMINATION

Isaiah 1:17 (ESV) says, "Learn to do good; seek justice, correct oppression; bring justice to the fatherless, plead the widow's cause."

Jim Crow laws were designed to keep black people oppressed and they are impacting the prevention of voting in African American communities.. If you can't vote, then your voice is silenced. Voting can bring change. In the past, some black community members have complained that the polls were broken and they didn't get a chance to cast their ballot. The number of days the polls were opened were restricted. Some laws have been passed to prevent people from passing out bottled water to those who have to stand in long lines to vote.[19] The goal is

19. McKay, Rich. "Georgia Bans Giving Water to Voters in Line under Sweeping

to make people uncomfortable. Elections need to be fair and every citizen has the right to vote.

Dear Heavenly Father,

Bless communities that have been discriminated against to have more polls in their neighborhoods. Overturn every unjust law on the federal level. Set voter standards nationwide so cities and states can't pass laws that suppress voters. We bind up every intimidation tactic in Jesus' name. Lord, bless your people to be bold as they stand for change. Thank You for answering this prayer in Jesus' name. Amen.

Restrictions." Reuters. March 25, 2021. Accessed July 06, 2021. https://www.reuters.com/article/us-usa-georgia-voting/georgia-bans-giving-water-to-voters-in-line-under-sweeping-restrictions-idUSKBN2BH2TC.

Sexism

S EXISM HAS BEEN A huge problem in America for decades. Many women were expected to stay at home and never have a career. They could only get domestic jobs and when they got jobs where males dominated, their pay was significantly less than men for doing the same jobs. There have been many cases of sexual harassment on the jobs and many women were unprotected. Our prayers are shifting things in this nation so women can do great exploits.

NO HATRED

Proverbs 10:12 (ESV) says, "Hatred stirs up strife, but love covers all offenses."

God is love and He commands us to love our neighbors as we love ourselves. It's not right to hate someone because of their gender. God has used women in a powerful way and He has anointed them more now than as never before. Women are more than sex objects or trophies. They are smart and talented. For this reason, God has created opportunities for women to access certain platforms and go through certain doors.

Dear Heavenly Father,

Lord uproot every false belief concerning women. Bless them to be respected in their community and in their jobs. Create opportunities for the overlooked. Lord, you used the weak to confound the mighty. Thank You for answering this prayer in Jesus' name. Amen.

PROTECTION

Psalm 72:4 (ESV) says, "May he defend the cause of the poor of the people, give deliverance to the children of the needy, and crush the oppressor!"

In certain streams, sexual harassment is horrendous. Some women don't know who to tell because they are afraid of losing their jobs. Some of the people around them need to be delivered from lust and respect their boundaries. Not only are women threatened physically but also financially. There needs to be equal pay, especially if they are doing the same job as their male peers and have the same skill or education level. God can turn things around and make every crooked place straight.

Dear Heavenly Father,

Heal every woman that has been violated and manipulated. Heal and deliver her from trauma and pain. We bind up any injustice and oppression in Jesus' name. Keep Your daughters safe from sexual predators and from those who want to

do them harm. Thank You for answering this prayer in Jesus' name. Amen.

Support

Ecclesiastes 4:12 (ESV) says, " And though a man might prevail against one who is alone, two will withstand him—a threefold cord is not quickly broken."

It does us no good if we are saving the world, but our homes are a mess. Some women sacrifice so much for their families, but they are met with a lot of resistance from their husbands. Their spouses don't want them to work or become jealous if they make more money. These women need supportive partners and help in their homes. God can cause their homes to be a peaceful place where His presence dwells.

Dear Heavenly Father,

You are so worthy. Send peace in every home where there is disorder. Line things up according to Your Word. We bind up domestic violence, sexual trauma, strife, jealousy, and chaos. Bless the husband and wife to love and cherish each other. Allow them to work together so they can excel and You can get the glory. Thank You for answering this prayer in Jesus' name. Amen.

Drug Addiction/All Addictions

MANY HAVE OPIOID, MARIJUANA, gambling, and other addictions. These have led to some people's demise and imprisonment. As people are bound, the enemy is running rampant in their lives. Jesus' Christ can set them free with His power.

DELIVERANCE

Psalm 34:17 (ESV) says, "When the righteous cry for help, the Lord hears and delivers them out of all their troubles."

God's power is stronger than the enemy's. Some people might need to get counseling or go to rehab to unlearn harmful behavior. However, God can transform us from the inside out. He will get to the root of the issue and deliver us with His power. We can find out the source of our bondage. Jesus is the savior that the world needs. Some are turning to drugs or other toxic behavior to fill their voids in their heart, but Jesus is the solution. As we continue praying, many will get saved as they turn from their wicked ways.

Dear Heavenly Father,

Give us strategies to witness to those who are addicted to drugs and other sinful activities. One plants. Another waters, but You give the increase. Bring forth a mighty harvest of souls. Fill every void in the people's heart that we cross paths with daily. Allow them to surrender all to You so their lives can be transformed out of darkness into Your marvelous light. Amen.

REMOVING IDOLS/ HINDRANCES

Matthew 4:10 (ESV) says, "Then Jesus said to him, "Be gone, Satan! For it is written, "'You shall worship the Lord your God and him only shall you serve.'"

Some people feel like they can't live their lives without their drugs or other things. Anything that we place before God is an idol and God is a jealous God. We should put nothing and no one before Him. Addictions can be harmful and hinder us in life. We know it's bad for us and we can't get free as we continue to feed harmful behaviors. As a result, there is a self-sabotaging spirit that causes people to destroy themselves. Jesus can destroy this spirit and prevent people from dying prematurely. We must pray that people let God in so their minds can be renewed and they can be in His will.

Dear Heavenly Father,

Remove idolatry and hindrances in our lives. Allow us not to be dependent on drugs or other harmful things. Bless us to trust You and depend fully on You. Bless us to forgive ourselves once we accept You into our hearts. Bless us to move forward in You so You can turn our mess into a message for Your glory. Thank You for answering this prayer in Jesus' name. Amen.

OVERCOME TEMPTATION

John 16:33 (ESV) says, "I have said these things to you, that in me you may have peace. In the world you will have tribulation. But take heart; I have overcome the world."

Jesus tells us to pray always, so we won't be led into temptation. Temptation is something that our flesh enjoys. However, we need to fall in love with Jesus, so we don't sin against Him. God will send people in our lives to hold us accountable. They aren't our enemies and we must take heed to their warning, so we don't fall back into sin. We can also put on the full armor of God (Ephesians 6), so we can stand against the wiles of the devil. Lastly, we can stand on God's Word and know that He will never leave or forsake us. Sin will not reign over us!

Dear Heavenly Father,

Strengthen our prayer life so we can overcome the temptation to do drugs or other sinful behaviors. Send us accountability partners who will tell us the truth even if it hurts our feelings. We bind up pride or rebellion so we can stay in Your will. Allow us to be equipped against all demonic attacks so we can withstand the enemy. We put on the full armor of God and we stand on Your Word. Thank You for answering this prayer in Jesus' name. Amen.

Climate

*T*HERE ARE MANY ENVIRONMENTAL issues and we must have the right policies in place to protect the landscape, animals, natural resources, water, and air. The climate has been affected due to a lot of carbon emissions in the atmosphere and the increasing size of the ozone layer.[20] Since the world is hotter, some of the icebergs in the arctic are melting and causing some animals to migrate south.

RIGHT LAWS

Isaiah 33:22 (ESV) says, "For the Lord is our judge; the Lord is our lawgiver; the Lord is our king; he will save us."

Some politicians could care less about the environment. They just focus on wealth and allow big corporations freedoms that further hurt the environment. Pollution or toxic waste from some factories needs to be regulated to ensure the safety of wildlife and the environment. Many people have gotten sick

---

20. "Is There a Connection Between the Ozone Hole and Global Warming?" Union of Concerned Scientists. Accessed July 06, 2021. https://www.ucsusa.org/resources/ozone-hole-and-global-warming.

due to harmful contaminants in the air, land, or water. There have been products that have cut carbon emissions, such as light bulbs. More laws need to be passed to protect the environment.

Dear Heavenly Father,

Raise up the right leaders and groups to advocate for the environment. Bless pollution to be cut down, so it doesn't do harm to the environment, water, land, air, animals. Put laws in place so people won't be so quick to litter. Bless people to take care of the public parks and communities. Allow more innovative products to be created to cut down on greenhouse gases or carbon emissions. Thank you for answering this prayer in Jesus' name. Amen.

ANIMALS

Matthew 6:26 (ESV) says, "Look at the birds of the air: they neither sow nor reap nor gather into barns, and yet your heavenly Father feeds them. Are you not of more value than they?"

Many animals are extinct and endangered. Some are hunted or outside of their natural habitat and can't survive. Sometimes animals have ingested plastics, glass, or wastes in the environment and gotten sick. For instance, when there is an oil spill in the ocean, many fish and birds get sick and perish. In livestock, some are being fed cancerous foods. When humans consume them, they become sick. There must be laws to protect our animals.

Dear Heavenly Father,

You created animals and it is not your will for them to be extinct. If they are endangered, allow them to multiple and thrive as never before. Bless hurt animals to go to wildlife sanctuaries so they can be treated and get the healing they need. Bless more laws to protect our animals to be passed. Thank You for answering this prayer in Jesus' name. Amen.

PROTECTION FROM ADVERSE WEATHER CONDITIONS

Psalm 91:11 (ESV) says, "For he will command his angels concerning you to guard you in all your ways."

Whenever there is a hurricane, tornado, hail, drought, fire, flood, etc. people suffer and so does the environment. Many people and animals are displaced from their homes. Crops are destroyed. Some people don't have insurance and are now faced with homelessness. They now need resources to survive. God can protect us from adverse weather. He can provide for all our needs.

Dear Heavenly Father,

You created animals and it is not your will for them to be extinct. If they are endangered, allow them to multiply and thrive as never before. Bless hurt animals to go to wildlife sanctuaries so they can be treated and get the healing they need. Bless more laws to protect our animals to be passed. Thank You for answering this prayer in Jesus' name. Amen.

DAY 20

Immigration

W HEN DONALD TRUMP WAS President, he restricted the number of immigrants who could enter our country. As a result, some families were separated and deported. Many immigrants were scared that Trump would deport them, so they stayed in hiding. When Joe Biden became President, many immigrants crossed the border and stayed in holding facilities that were crowded.[21]

PROTECTION

Psalm 32:7 (ESV) says, "You are a hiding place for me; you preserve me from trouble; you surround me with shouts of deliverance. Selah."

The journey for many immigrants to the United States is a dangerous one. They might have to travel for days with little to eat or drink. Some have to cross rivers that the current could sweep them upstream. Others have to climb over the tall wall that Donald Trump had built. Yet, they feel like the risk of leav-

---

21. Spagat, Elliot. "Over 4,000 Migrants, Many Kids, Crowded into Texas Facility." AP NEWS. March 31, 2021. Accessed July 06, 2021. https://apnews.com/article/joe-biden-immigration-texas-59d0eafb23d135f901dfc50ff326cfcd.

ing everything to come to America is worth it. God will protect them as they travel. Also, God will protect them from hate crimes.

UNIFIED WITH FAMILIES

1 Peter 3:8 (ESV) says, "Finally, all of you, have unity of mind, sympathy, brotherly love, a tender heart, and a humble mind."

One of the biggest struggles for immigrants is to be separated from their families. Some are located in the United States while their loved ones are back in their home country. Many immigrants get a job and send money to their families. Bless the immigrants to get any documents they need to become a citizen. God can unify their families, provide shelter, and prosper them.

Dear Heavenly Father,

Lord, please bless with just laws being passed concerning immigration. Provide shelter, prosperity, and allow them to develop a relationship with You. Lord, sustain them as they transition in life. Bless them to adjust well in Jesus' name. Amen.

Unemployment

*D*URING THE COVID-19 PANDEMIC, many jobs were cut and companies went bankrupt. Some people struggled to find work and were able to get unemployment benefits. However, some didn't want to go back to work because the unemployment paid more than their regular jobs. Nevertheless, God prospered His people, so they could have consistent income regardless of the economy crashing.

OPEN DOORS OF EMPLOYMENT

Revelation 3:8 says, "I know thy works: behold, I have set before thee an open door, and no man can shut it: for thou hast a little strength, and hast kept my word, and hast not denied my name."

God can open up doors that no man can shut. His promises are yes and amen. When things are stagnant, He will open up the heavens and provide. God will anoint applications to be seen out of many so our skill sets can be highlighted. He will give us favor with the interviewers, even causing us to be hired on the spot. God will make things happen for us if we continue to pray.

Dear Heavenly Father,

Bless those who need jobs to find employment. Allow the jobs to have great pay and benefits. Allow those struggling to be able to provide for their families. If people can't keep a job, break the cycle and bless them with stability. Thank You for answering this prayer in Jesus' name. Amen.

NO LOSS

Psalm 30:5 says, "For his anger endureth but a moment; in his favour is life: weeping may endure for a night, but joy cometh in the morning."

One of the biggest stresses of not having any income is that the bills will not get paid. There is a fear of being homeless, getting the vehicle repossessed, and not having any food. However, God can supernaturally provide and cause money, food, and supplies to come forth. He can break the curse of lack and provide for you and your families. He will even allow you to qualify for benefits with retroactive pay. Weeping may endure for a night, but joy comes in the morning.

Dear Heavenly Father,

Bless your people not to lose anything. Sustain them and break the curse of lack. You will supply all of our needs and give us trouble for our trouble. You daily load us with benefits and delight in the prosperity of your servants. Thank You for Your provision in Jesus' name. Amen.

Marriage

OVID-19 HAS PUT A lot of strain on some marriages. Domestic violence cases were trending due to the stress of everything.[22] God commanded the husband to love his wife as Christ loves the church. Wives are commanded to respect their own husbands. Love conquers all and can shift the environment to a peaceful one.

God can restore broken relationships because He has given us the ministry of reconciliation. There is nothing too hard for Him to fix.

UNITY

Colossians 3:14 (ESV) says, "And above all these put on love, which binds everything together in perfect harmony."

Husbands and wives are one flesh. They need to be unified in order to walk together. Teamwork makes the dream work. If

---

22. Nikos-Rose, Karen Michele. "COVID-19 Isolation Linked to Increased Domestic Violence, Researchers Suggest." UC Davis. March 01, 2021. Accessed July 06, 2021. https://www.ucdavis.edu/news/covid-19-isolation-linked-increased-domestic-violence-researchers-suggest.

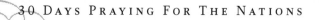

there are communication issues, God can work it out. The government is trying to refine marriage but God has established this institution from the beginning between a man and woman. As a result, people treat marriage as common but this is a covenant relationship. Divorce shouldn't be the first option. Marriage is a lifelong commitment. Husbands and wives can overcome every challenge through Jesus.

Dear Heavenly Father,

We bind up adultery, divorce, and domestic violence in marriages. Establish great communication and break off any generational curses. We bind up selfishness and the spirit of death. Allow husbands and wives to come together during stressful times. Bless them to pray and fast together, Allow them to enjoy each other's company. Thank You for answering this prayer in Jesus' name. Amen.

Abortion

*I*N 2019, ABORTION ISSUES surfaced. Some states passed full-term abortion laws, while other states banned it. As Christians prayed, things began to shift and wicked laws were overturned. Abortion is murder because the fetus has a heartbeat. There was a demonic agenda behind the increased cases of abortion. In Leviticus 18, people sacrificed their children to Molech. As we continue to pray, many eyes will be opened to the truth and unborn lives will be saved.

BIND UP UNJUST LAWS

Proverbs 17:15 (ESV) says, "He who justifies the wicked and he who condemns the righteous are both alike an abomination to the Lord."

The fervent effectual prayers of the righteous availeth much. Our prayers can penetrate the heavens and cause unjust laws to be overturned. God is raising up people to stand in front of abortion clinics to witness to those who are considering terminating their pregnancy. There are other options, such as adoption. Some women are being saved, delivered, and changed as they hear God's servants. God can turn people's hearts so they can change their minds.

Dear Heavenly Father,

We bind up spiritual wickedness in high places. Continue to send laborers in the field to witness to the loss and to those who are considering killing their unborn child. Heal every void in the mother's heart and show her other options. Thank You for answering this prayer in Jesus' name. Amen.

Wealth Gap/Injustice

THERE HAVE BEEN MANY laws to widen the gap between the poor and the rich. The pandemic has highlighted these issues and some members of Congress are considering reparations for African Americans. After slavery, they were promised 40 acres and a mule, but this promise was never executed by the government . Now, there are various politicians in the government trying to right wrongs.

MINORITIES TO HAVE WEALTH

Deuteronomy 8:18 (ESV) says, "You shall remember the Lord your God, for it is he who gives you power to get wealth, that he may confirm his covenant that he swore to your fathers, as it is this day."

It has been difficult for minorities to acquire wealth when there is discrimination. Some are denied loans, homes, scholarships, and jobs based on their skin color. Some don't receive fair opportunities for advancements, education, and don't have any generational wealth to leave to their children. Since Joe Biden has been elected President, there is talk of canceling student loans, first-time home buying assistance, and monthly stimulus checks to lessen the wealth gap.

Dear Heavenly Father,

Overturn laws that were created to suppress minorities. Bless there to be job and home equality. Establish wealth and riches in our house. Give us the wisdom to inquire about wealth and bless us to leave a legacy to our children's children. Allow every hole in our pockets to be closed. Thank You for answering this prayer in Jesus' name. Amen.

DAY 25

Taxes

PROVERBS 22:7 (ESV) SAYS, "The rich rules over the poor, and the borrower is the slave of the lender."

President Joe Biden wants to raise taxes on the rich because there are many loopholes where big corporations don't have to pay any taxes while the middle class and poor pay it all. President Biden wants these corporations to pay their share. Now is the time for the underdog to get ahead.

Dear Heavenly Father,

Overturn unfair tax laws that were meant to oppress the poor. We bind up oppression, poverty, and bondage. Lord, loose prosperity and expose corruption. Bless us with supernatural vindication for any wrong done against us. Bless us with supernatural provisions for those who have to pay back taxes but can't afford it. Thank You for answering this prayer in Jesus' name. Amen.

DAY 26

Homelessness

MATTHEW 8:20 (ESV) SAYS, "And Jesus said to him, "Foxes have holes, and birds of the air have nests, but the Son of Man has nowhere to lay his head."

Many cities have a huge homelessness problem because the cost of living is high or natural disasters left many displaced. Many sleep in the subway, parks, streets, dumpsters, cars, or hide in stores for shelter. Some cities have built tiny homes to combat this problem. God will make sure that we have a roof over our heads.

Dear Heavenly Father,

Bless the homeless to get back on their feet and have financial security. Allow them to be a good steward over wealth and to learn from their mistakes. Bless them to have a home of their own and money in their accounts. Break poverty and lack off of their lives. Allow them to be healthy. Bless them to get a great paying job and to seek You in the difficult times. Thank You for answering this prayer in Jesus' name. Amen.

Child Abuse

EPHESIANS 6:4 (ESV) SAYS, " Fathers, do not provoke your children to anger, but bring them up in the discipline and instruction of the Lord."

There are more horrific crimes committed against children daily. Children have been shot in their front yards, in their bedrooms, in the drive thru, and at the grocery store. The enemy desires to take out the next generation because they will make a great impact. School shootings have been so common. Our children need our prayers.

Dear Heavenly Father.

Place a hedge of protection around our children. We bind up death and every demonic agenda. Allow children to live in loving, peaceful homes and bless their caregivers to be delivered by your power. We come against sexual abuse, physical abuse, and emotional abuse. Bless the children to have a relationship with Jesus and heal them of any traumatic experiences. Send godly mentors in their lives to help them on this journey. Thank You for answering this prayer in Jesus' name. Amen.

Corruption

W**HAT IS DONE IN** the dark will be exposed in the light. Darkness can't overcome the light. It may seem like people are getting away with things. However, it will evenly catch up with them. God is not mocked. Whatever we sow, we will reap. Many financial schemes have been exposed. Those who were deceived later found out the truth of the corruption they were caught up in.

Dear Heavenly Father,

Expose corruption and fraud. Bless Your light to shine in darkness and overturn unjust laws. Remove wicked leaders and raise up godly leaders. We bind up treason, terrorism, stealing, cheating, killing, and sex trafficking. Loose integrity, honesty, purity, and righteousness. Bless people to turn their hearts back to You. Thank You for answering this prayer in Jesus' name. Amen.

LGBTQ

*L*EVITICUS 18:22 (ESV) SAYS, *"You shall not lie with a male as with a woman; it is an abomination."*

Homosexuality is a huge stronghold. The enemy is trying to push his agenda down our children's throats and loosing confusion about gender. Every truth that God establishes in His Word, the enemy perverts it. When God said there are only male and female for gender, the enemy is trying to establish many which is very confusing. Certain networks now promote LGBTQ+ agendas in cartoons and movies. The enemy is targeting education, media, feminine products, fashion, and so many areas.

Dear Heavenly Father,

Allow those bound by homosexuality to be saved and delivered. Remove any residue. Uproot demonic agendas in media, education, business, etc. Uproot perversion that entered the womb and through familial spirits. Bless those who are bound to realize that preaching the Gospel isn't a hate crime. Protect their eye and ear gates so they will keep their salvation and deliverance. Remove ungodly influences and uproot any false belief or teaching. Renew their minds with the Word of God. Thank You for answering this prayer in Jesus' name. Amen.

Business

*C*OLOSSIANS 3:23 (ESV) *says, "Whatever you do, work heartily, as for the Lord and not for men."*

Small businesses make up a lot of jobs and more people are becoming entrepreneurs. Since the pandemic, people have found creative ways to make money online. They had to learn how to adjust to a new normal. Most businesses were allowed to get funding from the government to pay rent, utilities, and payroll. God can prosper businesses.

Dear Heavenly Father,

Bless small businesses to prosper and Kingdom entrepreneurs to arise. Encourage business owners and allow them to have endurance. Give them wisdom and grace to run their business. Expand them so they can create jobs for others. Allow them to thrive during the pandemic or in the midst of a famine. Send clienteles from the north, south, east, and west. Thank You for answering this prayer in Jesus' name. Amen.

About The Author

KIMBERLY MOSES STARTED OFF her ministry as Kimberly Hargraves. She is highly sought after as a prophetic voice, intercessor and prolific author. There is no doubt that she has a global mandate on her life to serve the nations of the world by spreading the Gospel of Jesus Christ. She has a quickly expanding worldwide healing and deliverance ministry. Kimberly Moses wears many hats to fulfill the call God has placed on her life as an entrepreneur over several businesses including her own personal brand Rejoice Essentials which promotes the Gospel of Jesus Christ.

She also serves as a life coach and mentor to many women. She is also the loving mother of two wonderful children. She is married to Tron. Kimberly has dedicated her life to the work of ministry and to serve others under the call God has placed over her life. Kimberly currently resides in South Carolina.

She is a very anointed woman of God who signs, miracles and wonders follow. The miraculous and incessant testimonies attributed to her ministry are incalculable, with many reporting physical and mental healing, financial breakthroughs, debt cancellations and other favorable outcomes. She is known across the globe as a servant who truly labors on behalf of God's people through intercession.

She is the author of The Following:

"Overcoming Difficult Life Experiences with Scriptures and Prayers"
"Overcoming Emotions with Prayers"
"Daily Prayers That Bring Changes"
"In Right Standing,"
"Obedience Is Key,"
"Prayers That Break The Yoke Of The Enemy: A Book Of Declarations,"
"Prayers That Demolish Demonic Strongholds: A Book Of Declarations,"
"Work Smarter. Not Harder. A Book Of Declarations For The Workforce,"
"Set The Captives Free: A Book Of Deliverance."
"Pray More Challenge"
"Walk By Faith: A Daily Devotional"
"Empowering The New Me: Fifty Tips To Becoming A Godly Woman"
"School of the Prophets: A Curriculum For Success"
"8 Keys To Accessing The Supernatural"
"Conquering The Mind: A Daily Devotional"
"Enhancing The Prophetic In You"
"The ABCs of The Prophetic: Prophetic Characteristics"
"Wisdom Is The Principal Thing: A Daily Devotional"
"It Cost Me Everything"

"The Making Of A Prophet: Women Walking in Prophetic Destiny"

"The Art of Meditation: A Daily Devotional"

"Warfare Strategies: Biblical Weapons"

"Becoming A Better You"

"I Almost Died"

"The Pastor's Secret: The D.L. Series"

"June Bug The Busy Bee: The Gamer"

"June Bug The Busy Bee: The Bully"

"The Weary Prophet: Providing Practical Steps For Restoration"

"The Insignificant Woman"

"The Foolish Woman: A Daily Devotional"

"June Bug The Busy Bee: Sibling Rivalry"

"All Things Relationships"

"30 Day Pray For Your Spouse Challenge"

"The Christian Drama Queen Mentality"

You can find more about Kimberly at
www.kimberlyhargraves.com

For Rejoice Essential Magazine, visit
www.rejoiceessential.com

For beauty and t-shirts, visit
www.rejoicingbeauty.com

Please write a review for my books on Amazon.com

Support this ministry:
Cashapp: $ProphetessKimberly

Paypal.me/remag

Venmo: Kimberly-Moses-19

References

1. Leatherby, Lauren, Arielle Ray, Anjali Singhvi, Christiaan Triebert, Derek Watkins, and Haley Willis. "How a Presidential Rally Turned Into a Capitol Rampage." The New York Times. January 12, 2021. Accessed May 10, 2021. https://www.nytimes.com/interactive/2021/01/12/us/capitol-mob-timeline.html.

2. "Meaning of Numbers in the BibleThe Number 30." Bible Study. Accessed May 10, 2021. https://www.biblestudy.org/bibleref/meaning-of-numbers-in-bible/30.html.

3. "Trump Tells Woodward He Deliberately Downplayed Coronavirus Threat." NPR. September 10, 2020. Accessed May 10, 2021. https://www.npr.org/2020/09/10/911368698/trump-tells-woodward-he-deliberately-downplayed-coronavirus-threat.

4. Stolberg, Sheryl Gay. "Trump and Friends Got Coronavirus Care Many Others Couldn't." The New York Times. December 10, 2020. Accessed May 10, 2021. https://www.nytimes.com/2020/12/09/us/politics/trump-coronavirus-treatments.html.

5. "Kim Jong Un's Doctor Botched Heart Surgery as His Hands Were Shaking, Claims Report." Business Today.

April 26, 2020. Accessed May 10, 2021. https://www.businesstoday.in/latest/trends/kim-jong-uns-doctor-botched-heart-surgery-as-his-hands-were-shaking-claims-report/story/402055.html.

6. "Debt Cloud Hangs over Trump Post-presidency | The-Hill." Accessed May 10, 2021. https://thehill.com/policy/finance/534588-debt-cloud-hangs-over-trump-post-presidency.

7. Drescher, Jack. "On the 25th Amendment and Donald Trump: Don't Weaponize Psychiatry." Psychiatric News 56, no. 3 (2021). doi:10.1176/appi.pn.2021.3.37.

8. Norton, Jasmine Anderson/Allie. "Satanic Prayer at Council Meeting Disrupted by Crowd." WEAR. July 21, 2016. Accessed July 06, 2021. https://weartv.com/news/local/satanic-prayer-at-council-meeting-disrupted-by-crowd.

9. "Emmett Till." n.d. Biography. Accessed May 10, 2021. https://www.biography.com/crime-figure/emmett-till#:~:text=Murder%20Trial.

10. "Federal Judge Whose Son Was Killed in Ambush: 'My Son's Death Cannot Be in Vain.'" n.d. Www.cbsnews.com. Accessed May 10, 2021. https://www.cbsnews.com/news/esther-salas-son-murder-roy-den-hollander-48-hours/.

11. Hill, Evan. 2020. "How George Floyd Was Killed in Police Custody." The New York Times, May 31, 2020, sec. U.S. https://www.nytimes.com/2020/05/31/us/george-floyd-investigation.html.

12. reports, Staff and wire. n.d. "Death Penalty Sought in Florence Case Where 7 SC Officers Were Shot, 2 Fatally." Post and Courier. Accessed May 10, 2021. https://www.postandcourier.com/news/death-penalty-sought-

in-florence-case-where-7-sc-officers-were-shot-2-fatal-
ly/article_787386e0-acb4-11ea-8b77-93b85b6e72cf.
html#:~:text=Florence%20Police%20Sgt..

13. Leatherby, Lauren, Arielle Ray, Anjali Singhvi, Christiaan Triebert, Derek Watkins, and Haley Willis. 2021.
"How a Presidential Rally Turned into a Capitol Rampage." The New York Times, January 12, 2021, sec. U.S.
https://www.nytimes.com/interactive/2021/01/12/
us/capitol-mob-timeline.html.

14. "Christian Preacher Arrested for Saying That Homosexual Behavior Is a Sin." n.d. Adflegal.org. Accessed May
10, 2021. https://adflegal.org/blog/christian-preacher-
arrested-saying-homosexual-behavior-sin#close.

15. DAntonio, Michael, and Peter Eisner. "As Donald Trump
Faces Rising Dangers, 12 Religion Questions for Understudy Mike Pence." USA Today. September 13, 2018. Accessed July 06, 2021. https://www.usatoday.com/story/
opinion/2018/09/13/mike-pence-christian-first-how-
govern-president-donald-trump-column/1259832002/.

16. "Dr. Ben Carson - A Christian, First and Foremost."
Ohio Christian University. July 07, 2020. Accessed
July 06, 2021. https://www.ohiochristian.edu/news/
advancement/dr-ben-carson-christian-first-foremost.

17. "Is It Legal for Students to Pray in Public Schools?
| Freedom Forum Institute." n.d. Accessed May 10,
2021. https://www.freedomforuminstitute.org/
about/faq/is-it-legal-for-students-to-pray-in-public-
schools/#:~:text=Contrary%20to%20popular%20
myth%2C%20the.

18. Corasaniti, Nick. 2021. "Georgia G.O.P. Passes Major Law to Limit Voting amid Nationwide Push." The New York Times, March 25, 2021, sec. U.S. https://www.nytimes.com/2021/03/25/us/politics/georgia-voting-law-republicans.html.

19. McKay, Rich. "Georgia Bans Giving Water to Voters in Line under Sweeping Restrictions." Reuters. March 25, 2021. Accessed July 06, 2021. https://www.reuters.com/article/us-usa-georgia-voting/georgia-bans-giving-water-to-voters-in-line-under-sweeping-restrictions-idUSKBN2BH2TC.

20. "Is There a Connection Between the Ozone Hole and Global Warming?" Union of Concerned Scientists. Accessed July 06, 2021. https://www.ucsusa.org/resources/ozone-hole-and-global-warming.

21. Spagat, Elliot. "Over 4,000 Migrants, Many Kids, Crowded into Texas Facility." AP NEWS. March 31, 2021. Accessed July 06, 2021. https://apnews.com/article/joe-biden-immigration-texas-59d0eafb23d135f901df-c50ff326cfcd.

22. Nikos-Rose, Karen Michele. "COVID-19 Isolation Linked to Increased Domestic Violence, Researchers Suggest." UC Davis. March 01, 2021. Accessed July 06, 2021. https://www.ucdavis.edu/news/covid-19-isolation-linked-increased-domestic-violence-researchers-suggest.

Index

Egypt, 15

election, 5, 13, 40, 45, 117

emergency, 39, 41

Emmett Till, 20

emotions, 110

encourage, 42, 48, 115

encouragement, 41, 74, 100

enemy, 2, 12, 27, 31, 45, 46, 47, 48, 53, 55, 59, 60, 61, 62, 64, 68, 73, 74, 82, 84, 89, 90, 94, 95, 98, 99, 100, 101, 123, 126, 143, 145

entertainment,, 5, 52

environment, 8, 12, 17, 33, 47, 85, 88, 95, 105, 127, 128, 129, 135

equipment, 35, 114

ethnicities, 37, 77

evicted, 16

evil, 6, 13, 15, 17, 19, 22, 23, 24, 29, 35, 38, 48, 52, 73, 84, 87, 90, 92, 94, 99, 100, 101, 103, 104, 105

evil work, 13, 15, 52, 103, 104, 105

exams, 88

excellence, 30, 41

exercise, 7, 29, 91

exposes, 22, 109, 114

exposure, 16

extinct, 128, 129

eye, 10, 13, 36, 145

F

Facebook, 60

faint, 33

faith, 25, 34, 46, 59, 62, 63, 64, 66, 67, 74, 76, 87, 99, 103

faithful, 33, 35, 43, 53, 81, 90

faithfulness, 19

false deity, 108

false religion, 29, 107

fame, 6, 13, 73

families, 20, 24, 32, 33, 40, 42, 43, 88, 97, 104, 106, 122, 130, 131, 133

family, 5, 20, 24, 28, 32, 33, 44

famine, 15, 59, 147

faults, 2, 3

fear, 13, 17, 29, 30, 37, 41, 47, 54, 61, 65, 84, 88, 90, 97, 117, 133

fight, 9, 13, 19, 20, 21, 28, 34, 39, 48, 66, 91

finances, 35, 78

financial breakthroughs, 95, 148

financial stewards, 35

financial troubles, 9

financially, 21, 78, 121

First Amendment, 22, 66

first responders, 39

flesh, 29, 49, 52, 89, 125, 135

flint, 28, 41

floods, 96

Florence, 39

flu, 91

food industry, 92

Food recalls, 92

food safety, 4

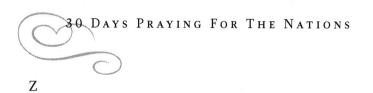

Z